Advance Prais

HOW TO WRITE WHAT YOU LOVE

"A decade ago, I attended my first writer's workshop as a nervous neophyte in need of encouragement. Dennis Hensley was my instructor and believe me, he delivered! Now his enthusiasm, energy, and encyclopedia of ideas are captured in print. If you've always wanted to do something with your writing, here's how to get going!"

—LIZ CURTIS HIGGS, best-selling author

"Dennis Hensley knows writing. He knows writers. He knows publishing. He knows publishers. He knows how to teach writing. He knows how to coach and inspire writers. He writes what he knows, and he knows—better than anyone I can imagine—how to write what you love...and make a living at it."

—BOB HOSTETLER, author and speaker

"This book is a *must read* for anybody wanting to make a living as a writer. A practical, no nonsense, nuts-and-bolts approach."

—BILL MYERS, author and film director

"In this practical, readable book, the prolific Dennis Hensley encourages aspiring freelancers and offers valuable suggestions gleaned from his years as a successful writer. I'll recommend it to my writer friends and students."

—VICKI HESTERMAN, PH.D., author, photographer, and college journalism professor

"As usual, Dennis Hensley nails it. Good solid advice from one who knows."

—JAMES RIORDAN, best-selling author of a dozen books

"Dennis Hensley is truly a motivator. His chatty, writer-to-writer tone, established on page one, removes fear, builds confidence, and will cause readers to say, 'Yes! I can do this.' With wit, wisdom, and candor, he unselfishly shares his decades of experience with newcomers to the field. His advice should save them much pain and postage."

—HOLLY G. MILLER, contributing editor for *Clarity* magazine and travel editor for the *Saturday Evening Post*

How to Write What You Love | and make a living at it

How to Write What You Love

| and make a living at it

DENNIS E. HENSLEY, PH.D.

SHAW

WATERBROOK
PRESS

How to Write What You Love and Make a Living at It
A SHAW BOOK
PUBLISHED BY WATERBROOK PRESS
2375 Telstar Drive, Suite 160
Colorado Springs, CO 80920
A division of Random House, Inc.

All Scripture quotations, unless otherwise indicated, are taken from *The Holy Bible, New International Version*®. NIV®. Copyright © 1973, 1978, 1984 by International Bible Society. Used by permission of Zondervan Publishing House. All rights reserved.

This book and the advice offered here is not intended to substitute for professional legal or accounting services. The advice is offered by a layperson who has made his living in writing. Be sure to consult an attorney or an accountant when issues arise.

ISBN 0-87788-174-X

Library of Congress Cataloging-in-Publication Data

Hensley, Dennis E. 1948–
    How to write what you love...and make a living at it / Dennis Hensley.
      p. cm.
    ISBN 0-87788-174-X (pbk.)
   1. Authorship. 2. Journalism—Authorship. 3. Feature writing. 4. Freelance journalism.
I. Title.

PN147 .H3755   2000
808'.06607—dc21   00-037380

Printed in the United States of America
2000—First Edition

10 9 8 7 6 5 4 3 2 1

*This book is affectionately dedicated
to the one person who, since childhood,
has encouraged me to write on and on:
my brother, Gary A. Hensley…
accountant, journalist, writer, pal.*

CONTENTS

ACKNOWLEDGMENTS

I wish to thank Joan Guest of Harold Shaw Publishers for believing in this book project and for her constant encouragement. I wish to thank Pamela Rice Hahn for helping me through the technical formatting of this manuscript. Additional thanks go to my friend and colleague Dr. Pam Jordan, chair of the Taylor University Fort Wayne English department, who helped me develop the Professional Writing major for our campus. The major puts into practice many of the concepts found in this text. And finally, a tip of the hat goes to longtime writer and editor friends who have encouraged me for many years: Lin Johnson, Bill Myers, Jim Riordan, Holly G. Miller, Bob Hostetler, Clare Seffrin Bond, Reg Forder, Peter Rubie, Rick Hill, Jerry Jenkins, Liz Curtis Higgs, Earl Conn, Joan Alexander, John Ingrisano, Michael Smith, Jim Watkins, Sally E. Stuart, Janette Oke, Steve Laube, Michael Landon, Jr., and Linda McGinn.

FOREWORD

Dennis E. Hensley's word processor must be wired for 220 volts! This energetic author has not only written thirty-one books, ghostwritten eighteen other books, and sold more than 3,000 freelance articles, but he also manages to be a popular university professor and writers' conference speaker.

His high-voltage seminars, now captured herein, will energize your writing and freelance career—even if you're not a human dynamo.

Though I'm wired for much lower voltage than my friend Dennis, I've used his principles and have published eleven books and some 1,200 articles— all while maintaining a busy speaking schedule and managing to have a family life.

This latest book shares Hensley's secrets for becoming a successful freelance writer: what to write about, how to write with a distinctive style, how to land a literary agent or negotiate your own contract, and so much more. This "wired" book is both highly motivational and, at the same time, extremely practical.

So, start turning pages and get charged up!

—Jim Watkins

PREFACE

When I originally wrote the text of my first book about professional writing, *The Freelancer,* back in 1985, word processors were new and the Internet had not even been thought of. Today, you cannot write for a target market without being aware of all the opportunities available in both the standard print media and the on-line media. That is why I've had a strong desire to write this new book. Many of the basic lessons found in my six earlier books on writing regarding writing, editing, proofreading, researching, interviewing, and marketing are still valid; so, they are condensed and included in this text. However, all of these sections have now been enhanced to include insights into the world of on-line capabilities.

Whereas magazine formats may have changed during the past few decades, the fact remains that computers and word processors have not replaced the writer's role in the communication network. Computers don't dream, but writers do. Computers don't fantasize, but writers do. Computers don't write jokes or act out scenes or cry or scream or feel love or anger, but writers do.

In truth, the only real *word processor* is still the human brain. That is why this book also focuses on writing we just "like" to do, even if it does not involve an assignment from an editor or an attempt to get published.

This book has been written to help you focus that personal word processor of yours (your marvelous brain) on an adventure in writing. You will be shown how to write and then how to sell what you write. If you have the desire to write, I have the techniques to show you how to do that.

Read now and enjoy becoming a writer.

—*Dr. Dennis E. Hensley*

PART I

Becoming a Freelance Writer

Three millennia ago Solomon noted, "Of making many books there is no end" (Ecclesiastes 12:12). He meant this as a lament. Here was a man who was seeking solace and comfort from books, yet he found pages filled only with random words, empty examples, and hollow stories. Surely this is a legacy no writer would want to leave.

The conscientious writer chooses topics for the takeaway value they will have to the reader, and not just for the sales those topics will generate. If you set your standards for high takeaway value in your manuscript, that means your reader will experience some growth or other benefit from that reading experience.

If you have thought about sitting down and dashing off a book about your life or work or interests, it's time to think again. Professional writing cannot be dashed off. It's hard work.

For it to be legitimate and valuable, it must be contemporary, solid, precise, and interesting. Modern readers have huge expectations. Meeting such expectations is a challenge. Let me explain why this is true.

CHAPTER ONE

The Challenge of Writing

Robert Louis Stevenson was once asked if he loved to write. He replied, "I hate to write, but I love to have written."

Anyone who has ever tried to work as a freelance writer understands Stevenson's sentiments. It's a joy to see your byline in print, to receive a royalty check in the mail, and to get compliments from people who are enthusiastic about things you have written. However, getting to that stage of the game is the rough part. At times, a blank computer screen can be intimidating. Freelance writing is a very challenging career and one that should not be jumped into by starry-eyed individuals.

Writing is one of the oldest of all professions. As far back as Old Testament times, Job lamented, "Oh, that my words were written! Oh, that they were inscribed in a book!" (Job 19:23). Fortunately for the new writer, there is a wealth of recorded experience to draw upon. Novice writers can study the lessons passed on by the masters and, in so doing, avoid certain pitfalls. Just as we can learn by doing, we can also learn by reading what others have done.

What do all writers have in common? Although writing styles may vary greatly, the bedrock foundations of good writing—proper grammar, well-structured syntax, varied vocabulary, accurate spelling, and correct punctuation—never change. These are constants in the writing profession.

That's not all. The basic approaches to good writing are also standard and firm. One basic tenet was provided by Epictetus, the Greek philosopher, who said almost two thousand years ago, "If you want to be a writer, write." That is still good advice. More recently, Joseph Pulitzer added to that starting point: "Put it before them briefly so they will read it, clearly so they will appreciate it, picturesquely so they will remember it and, above all, accurately so they will be guided by its light." That, too, is good advice. Both Epictetus and Pulitzer knew that the art of writing takes a certain type of discipline.

But if the foundations of and approaches to good writing do not change from one age to the next, something else certainly does. That something is the freelance writer. Writers change because their professional environment is constantly being altered.

Consider equipment, for example. The transfers from stylus to quill to pencil to ink pen to ballpoint pen to typewriter to computer have altered the writer's approach to his or her labors over the centuries. With each advance the author's mind has become freer of the more tedious aspects of writing and has been able to produce more copy at a faster rate. What took an apostle weeks to transcribe can now be put to paper in less than an hour.

Even paper has changed writers' work. Papyrus was not only harder to write on than 20-pound bond, but it was also harder to come by and costlier. Thus, first drafts and multiple rewrites are fairly recent writing innovations. Today's writer can do a rough draft in word processing without using any paper at all, while allowing him or herself to experiment with approaches and styles. Previous generations could not indulge in such luxuries.

Changes in laws have affected writers, too. Charles Dickens did not have the protection of the international copyright system enjoyed by today's authors; much of Dickens's time was spent campaigning for his rights rather than writing. Thomas Paine was not protected by the First Amendment right to freedom of speech; he spent as much of his time avoiding the king's agents as he did writing and printing pamphlets. We have neither of these worries today.

Even changes in the marketing of manuscripts have influenced freelance writers. Daniel Defoe used to write and print his own tracts and booklets and then personally sell them from door to door. Today's writer works with literary agents, private publishing companies, and advertising firms. Thoughts about paperback rights, reprints, book club selections, serializations, and movie sales are recent developments that Chaucer, Bunyan, Shakespeare, Milton, and Cervantes never had to contemplate.

The examples of change are endless. However, the bottom line is this: Each era has its own special problems and challenges for the working writer. Good writing and approaches to good writing have constants, but the psychological, professional, and financial aspects of being a professional writer are modified from one age to the next. Only the creative commitment remains the same.

To face the current publishing markets, you will need to develop the attributes of today's successful writers. Let me get you started by explaining what marks these writers as special.

FREELANCER TRAITS

Have you ever wondered why editors often give the majority of their freelance assignments to a select group, or "stable," of freelance writers? The answer is obvious. These writers have the traits those editors look for in writers. If you can develop the same traits, you, too, can be equally as busy. An editor who trusts and respects you becomes your advocate and sponsor.

Endurance
Do you have the tenacity to see an assignment through to the end? Some assignments can get tedious, even boring, but you must always honor your promise to deliver a finished manuscript.

Versatility
Can you cover hard news, write features, conduct interviews, report on meetings, do legwork research, and take photographs, too? If so, you can handle virtually any available assignment. The more you are capable of doing, the more chances an editor will have to seek your services. Always continue to expand your writing (and related) skills.

Initiative
Are you a self-starter who needs a minimum amount of direct supervision? Editors expect you to be a confident and independent worker. Remember that your job is to relieve the editor of work, not to provide new burdens.

Sensitivity

Do you have tact and patience in order to deal with people effectively (whether you are interviewing them, asking them for information, or simply trying to explain to them why you need a statement "for the record")? Good writers are people-oriented and know how to empathize with other people's concerns and needs.

Integrity

Can you present all sides? It is not enough just to report the news accurately. It also must be presented without bias. You must tell both sides of the story, present all pertinent information, and offer an honest overview of any circumstance. Telling the whole truth about half the facts is slanted reporting. Responsible editors cannot condone this.

Efficiency

Have you learned to get the complete story? Before moving on to a new assignment, get all the photos, quotations, sidebar material, and background information possible on the current assignment.

Experience

Do you have a good balance between formal education and school-of-hard-knocks training? If so, editors will appreciate you. The more you've done, the more you've traveled, and the more you've studied, the more valuable you become to an editor. To be a powerful writer, you need depth of experience. Live life before you try to explain it to readers.

Creativity

Are you innovative? Do you take a unique approach to your work? You will keep an editor interested in you. You need to come up with unusual topics to cover; you need to be able to write clever leads; you must develop a sixth sense about what people like to read about, learn about, talk about.

Timeliness

Can you meet or beat a deadline? (Remember what deadline means: "Go past this line, and you're dead.") The ability to meet deadlines assures your editor that you are reliable and professional.

Zest

Do you have the enthusiasm it takes? Editors enjoy working with upbeat, positive-thinking writers who have good communication skills, good work habits, and a good sense of humor. If these are traits of your personality, you will have an edge over many other writers.

As you review this list of traits, test yourself against them. Do you lack some of these qualities? Perhaps you have some, but not to the degree of professionalism you would like.

The solution is to concentrate on one trait at a time and to enhance your ability in that area. For example, if you lack versatility, challenge yourself to change that. How? Attend more writers' conferences and workshops; keep up-to-date on the articles published in writing trade journals; and read more books about writing. After you do those things, practice the new skills you've been challenged by until you do become more versatile.

Editors who are burdened by heavy workloads and pressured by demanding deadlines find it desirable to call on a reliable freelancer to handle some of the pending assignments. If you can prove to an editor that you have the traits of a good freelancer, you will find steady work coming your way.

WRITERS' CONFERENCES

Developing good freelance traits does not have to be done alone. You can get career guidance, classroom instruction, and manuscript editing at dozens of writers' conferences held annually around the country. Conferences are great opportunities for networking with editors and agents, as well.

I floundered on my own for almost three years as a fledgling freelance writer before I attended my first five-day writers' conference. The three years were poorly spent; the five days were well invested. After that first conference, my writing career began to advance by great strides.

Today, many years and many bylines later, I still attend conferences. These days, however, I'm one of the instructors. Nevertheless, I continue to find the same value and excitement in conferences that I found during those early years. When it comes to meeting interesting new people, enjoying good fellowship, gathering new writing ideas, discovering new publishing markets, becoming familiar with new styles and formats of writing, or just getting away for some relaxing travel, nothing matches a well-planned writers' conference.

Unfortunately, very few people know how to make the best use of their time at a writers' conference. Getting your money's worth out of a conference is like getting your money's worth out of a vacation; it takes careful selection and planning and preparation.

Begin by selecting a conference best suited to your needs. Decide this by asking friends in your local writing club or joining an on-line writers' chat room or calling area college English professors and asking about the conferences they have attended. You may also write to several conference directors for free descriptive brochures. Usually, by figuring in advance how much money you will have to spend on travel and tuition, you will be able to narrow the choices rapidly. Study the conference programs for quality content (make sure there are plenty of lectures by reputable instructors) and emphasis (some conferences offer something for everyone, whereas others focus strictly upon inspirational writing or poetry or journalism, so make sure you find one to meet your needs).

Don't be too hasty to rule out a conference several hundred miles from your home. If you are a working writer—even a beginner—some of your conference expenses will be tax deductible. Furthermore, you might be able to sell travel features to your hometown newspaper about the out-of-state location you will be visiting. Many conferences also provide full or partial scholarships, or they provide cash prizes through writing contests.

The most important consideration is this: Will you be getting the kind of help you need for your particular writing interests? The extra money spent in travel will come back to you once you learn how to increase your manuscript sales. So, invest a little, plan a lot, and expect a good return.

Once you have selected a conference, be sure to go to it with all necessary materials in hand. You will need pencils, ink pens, notepads, and a cassette recorder (for recording lectures in class and conducting interviews with guest authors out of class). Take plenty of cassette tapes and spare batteries. You may also want to bring your laptop. Many conferences have hookups for laptop computers for use in class or in the dorm or hotel rooms.

If you have business cards or vita sheets, take plenty to exchange with other writers or to give to editors and publishers at the conference. Also, take along a book or two to read during the evenings when you are trying to unwind after a hectic day of classes and workshops. Many workshops provide handouts, such as magazine guidelines or sample issues, so be sure to take along an extra tote bag to use to transport those items back home.

Most important of all, take at least three different manuscripts you have completed. Some conferences arrange informal swap-and-critique sessions in which you and your fellow conference registrants can read and analyze one anothers' manuscripts.

At the conference, sign up for a private counseling session with one of the conference instructors or an editor-in-residence or a literary agent and bring those manuscripts along. They will want to examine your writings. Here you can talk face to face with people whom you've had trouble reaching by mail.

When you arrive at your conference, be quick about working the crowd. Look at nametags and find people from other states. Ask them to tell you about their regional publications, about the freelance policies of the large newspapers in their states, and about any writing workshops or conferences coming up in their areas.

If you are looking for a coauthor for a book or article, place a note on the workshop bulletin board right away. Explain your project and list your home and temporary conference addresses, your e-mail address, and your phone and fax numbers.

During breakfast or lunch on the first day, strike up a conversation with someone who will be attending classes you won't be in. Work out a deal: Tell that person you will trade the notes from your classes on poetry and playwriting for copies of his or her notes from the classes on short story and novel writing. By doing this, you will make a new friend, double your amount of notes, and save time and money. Or take along an additional microcassette recorder and plenty of blank tapes and ask that person to tape his or her classes for you.

Even when attending your own class sessions, record your instructor's lectures. Tapes are valuable for the following reasons:

1. The memory cannot retain everything it hears. Tapes miss nothing.
2. With the tape "taking notes" for you (which you can play back over and over once you are home), your mind will be free to concentrate more on the lecture, on questions raised by members of the class, and on the notes or charts your teacher will be presenting.
3. Tapes allow you the freedom to write memos of other sorts, such as follow-up questions to ask the teacher out of class.

It should be noted, however, that some instructors who have contracts for books with their publishers and, thus, have their lectures copyrighted, will not permit tape-recording during their lectures. Usually, they will have audiotapes for sale, however.

After you have been to an instructor's workshop, you may want to sign up for a private session to discuss your manuscript as well as ideas he or she brought up in class. What do you need to know in order to prepare for a private session?

Be professional. Be businesslike and thorough when you go to that private session.

Bring questions. Have your list of questions ready about things said in the workshop about which you need more clarification. (It's best to keep your questions in class limited to ones whose answers will benefit all of those in attendance. Ask the questions more particular to your writing during your private sessions.)

Target your specific needs. Make sure that when you offer your manuscript for discussion, you bring a list of specific questions about it. Don't ask general questions: "Are my characters believable?" or "Do you think my plot is interesting?" Instead, ask, "How can I improve my dialogue sequence here on page nine?" or "Can you help me rework my lead paragraph so that it will have a better narrative hook?"

Go over problem sections of your manuscript. Use your teacher to help you edit places in your manuscript that have never worked for you in your rewrites.

Prepare a sample query letter. Bring a sample query letter for selling your manuscript to a publisher and have the teacher examine that, too.

Sometimes you can "stretch" your private session with your instructor by making a follow-up appointment of a more social nature. Just say, "If you're free between your two class lectures tomorrow afternoon, I'd like to buy you a cup of coffee and talk a little more about how you outline your books before you write them." Most instructors (including me) never tire of talking shop and usually will be happy to accept invitations for chats over coffee or a meal.

Attending a conference is fun, but taking advantage of all the things available to you requires strategy and planning on your part.

If you go to a conference with the goal of gaining enough information to keep you busy with follow-up research and projects for several months, you will come away with more than your money's worth in ideas, contacts, and experiences.

ACCEPTING CRITICISM

One thing you may find difficult to accept at a writers' conference will be the critiquing of your work. However, if you really want to succeed as a writer, you will seek a thorough editing of your manuscripts. After all, you don't have time to waste. You want to know just what to correct and what to leave as it is. That requires tough editing, and tough editing leads to quick learning.

Trust me, I know what I'm talking about. I have a Ph.D. in English, but nine years of college didn't teach me as much about writing as two months did with a no-nonsense literary agent and six months with a hard-nosed newspaper editor.

As a novice writer, you should learn about editing at the same time you learn about writing. That will gear you up to accept constructive editing help. Where do you begin? Spend time reading magazines and books on how to write. Self-study expands abilities, provides foundational information, and offers a continual review of previously learned skills.

But the best (and fastest) learning comes from the honest critics. If you are really in a hurry to refine your work and get it published, find yourself the most blunt and talented editor around and get that person to chew your copy to pieces. That's seems harsh, I know, but it's also a great truth.

People will tell you that a creative mind is a budding writer's greatest asset. Not so. It's a turtle-shell hide that makes you great. If you can endure the assault—if you can keep quiet and heed what you are being shown and taught—you will make incredible advancements in your writing career.

The pampered, wound-licking, would-be author who takes manuscript criticism as a personal affront will never advance very far. The writer who separates the *written* piece from the *writer* of the piece and allows the manuscript to be critiqued is the person who won't make the same mistakes twice. That's progress. It's also professionalism.

The real pro is someone who is completely open to suggestions for improvement. To me, the mark of a professional writer is a fanaticism about wanting to become better and better.

It's a trait I've seen in my friend Jonellen Heckler, who wrote her first novel, *Safekeeping* (G. P. Putnam's Sons), after a long reign as the most popular short story writer in the *Ladies' Home Journal*. Her novel received rave reviews, became a Literary Guild selection, was sold for translation in Norway and Germany, and was later mass-marketed as a paperback book.

While on a sixteen-state talk-show tour to promote the book, Jonellen and her husband spent three days with my family and me at our home. One evening, while going over *Safekeeping* with Jonellen, I showed her what I felt were especially fine passages of description, dialogue, and character development. She was grateful for that input.

I then pointed out that in an early chapter of the book she had described her main character as a sturdy woman with "steel bones." It was an effective image. Unfortunately, nine chapters later she had her character push her way through a crowd by first "steeling herself" for the elbowing and jolting, something that a person with steel bones should not have to do: resteel herself.

Jonellen took the book from me, read the passages back and forth, then put the book down. "Doggone it!" she said. "And we proofed this thing seven times before it went to press."

That response made a lasting impression on me. Jonellen didn't offer an excuse or call me a nitpicker or laugh it off. She accepted the criticism as valid, painful, and useful. That was one writing error she would never repeat.

I receive similar responses (though not nearly as often as I would like) at writers' conferences when I work one-on-one with my students. Some conference participants are there only for praise for their "masterpieces." They are the ones who go home disappointed and unenlightened. Others, however, are like the person who said to me, "Be blunt. I'm only here for five days. Don't waste time being tactful. I'm here to learn why my manuscripts keep getting rejected." Writers like that are sure bets for eventual success.

A writer should strive for perfection. The days of the handholding editors such as Maxwell Perkins, who would work through four or five drafts of a manuscript with authors like Hemingway and Fitzgerald, are long gone. Not many editors have the time to work with you step by step. And counting on your editor to do something by saying, "That's the editor's job," is the lazy writer's approach. Accept criticism when it comes and learn from it.

My first cold bath in manuscript criticism came when I was a twenty-three-year-old graduate student. I had written five chapters of a novel and had sent them to a literary agent who had been recommended to me by one of my professors.

After three weeks of waiting nervously, I received the first chapter from the agent. Stapled atop it was a handwritten memo that read, "You have a fabulous plot here, kid, but you don't know beans about style. Want to learn?" The enclosed chapter was a bloodbath of red ink. I felt ill. I was a moron, an idiot, a fool, a *failure.*

Shamefacedly, I showed the memo and chapter to my professor. She offered her congratulations and told me I probably had a real future in writing. That agent hadn't accepted a new client in more than six years, she explained.

To be honest, he didn't really accept me either. But we did correspond regularly for two months, and he butchered the other chapters. The agent showed me where my story rambled, where there were passages in need of more description, and where the dialogue was wooden. He was concise and accurate.

After the initial shock and numbness wore off, I actually began to get excited about all the "secrets" I was being shown. I paid close attention, and my writing improved. That first novel never sold, but I did later sell more than thirty other books. Strangely, I now know that that brutal editing gave me an edge on my classmates who had not had such an experience. My grades improved, my confidence increased, my writing matured.

But that was fiction writing. I learned how to be a journalist when I took a part-time job at the *Muncie Star* and worked under a stern-faced martinet who had all the charm of a sunburned gorilla. This guy not only stabbed you; he also twisted the knife. He lost reporters the way old men lose hair. And if I hadn't needed schooling money so desperately, I probably would have deserted him, too.

But I stayed. And my fear of the man's sharp tongue made me more careful about what I wrote. I listened attentively as that editor blue-penciled my copy and explained why my lead was a snore, why my quotes were incorrectly balanced in the article, and why my ending lacked snap. I smiled resolutely whenever I was sent back to the typewriter for a second, third, sometimes even a fourth draft of an article.

The man never praised anyone. After six months he was transferred to one of the chain's sister papers in Phoenix. I can't say I really missed him. But to give him his due, I must admit that the guy really did know about journalism. That editor did more to improve my writing in those six months than all of my college English professors had accomplished in six years. *They* had been concerned with the artistic flair of literature, but the newspaper editor had been concerned about *communicating*. I soon learned that the editor had the right idea. If you can't communicate, you can't survive as a writer.

You're already aware that the world is full of critics. Come up with an idea and ten critics will be ready to tell you why it won't work. That's not what you need. Critics are evaluators, but editors are teachers. There is a big difference. What you need are *teachers*.

An evaluator will look at your manuscript and say, "It doesn't set my soul aflame!" An editor will look at the same manuscript and say, "Burn it!"

Do not seek *emotional* responses to your manuscripts. That is what some critics offer. Save that for the postpublication assessments. What you need during the writing stage are helpful judgments of specifics: grammar, syntax, vocabulary, paragraph structure, and content. As Thornton Wilder noted, "If you master your techniques, literature will take care of itself." A good editor will help you move toward producing good literature.

How do you find a good editor? If you are in a writers' critique group or a writers' club, gravitate toward those members with the best track records in sales. Find someone who also has good editing skills and then woo that person. Take her to lunch one day, give her a nice gift (a novel, perhaps), and then explain your problem.

Say, "Jenny, I've got two kids at home and a husband who works nights. I want to be a writer, but there's no way I can go back to college. I need your help. I know you're busy with your own career, but I also know you have a willingness to help new writers. I've got a suitcase filled with rejected manuscripts. If you'll read a few and give them a thorough editing, I promise you I'll rework them and get them back in the mail. I'm not thin-skinned. I can accept harsh evaluations. In fact, I desperately need them. Right now, I don't even know what I'm doing wrong. How about it? Could we meet for lunch—my treat— for the next three Tuesdays and go over some of my manuscripts?"

In all likelihood, Jenny will identify with your dilemma, having been through it herself. She will probably consent; but if she is unable to, then seek someone else. Keep trying. Don't be reserved or shy about securing a tough editor for yourself. There are numerous ways you can go about it.

You can take a part-time position as a reporter for a weekly newspaper. You can ask your writer friends to recommend night school writing teachers at your local community college and then enroll in the class taught by the most rigid and exacting of the teachers.

You can attend a one-week writers' conference during the summer. Sign up for as many private critique sessions with your instructor as possible, and also get involved in the student-group manuscript evaluation times. You might even consider hiring one of the reputable writing critique services advertised in national writers' magazines and attach a cover letter with your submissions explaining that you want no punches pulled in the evaluations. Another idea would be to make contact with a literary agent who specializes in first novels or new writers and ask for assistance in shaping your manuscript. But keep in mind that these services can sometimes be expensive.

Once you find someone willing to be your teacher and taskmaster, here's what you need to do:
- Maintain a cooperative relationship with that individual.
- Accept criticism willingly.

- Be prompt for all appointments.
- Express your gratitude.
- Master the skills being taught to you.
- Ask questions about anything unclear to you, but don't talk otherwise.
- Don't explain or defend or apologize for what you have written; simply accept what is said about it and then revise the manuscript accordingly.
- Keep submitting manuscripts to publishers as you go; a sale will be as encouraging to your mentor as it will be to you.

More than anything else, *don't get discouraged.* Keep writing and marketing. Maintain your perspective. You are not a failure; you are a beginner and you're a learner. It is your *manuscript* that is being judged, not *you.* The more rigorous and accurate the judgment, the faster you will improve. And improvement is what it's all about.

UNDERSTAND THY PUBLISHING EDITOR

Once you have been through this developmental season of working with editors as teachers, mentors, and critics, you will begin to sell your work. Once that happens you will start to relate to editors professionally as they edit your magazine articles or books.

You need to keep your writing in perspective, but it's also important to keep your editor and his or her work in perspective. If you can learn what editors do, what they are looking for in a manuscript, and how you can assist in filling those needs, your working relationship with any editor will be greatly enhanced.

Remember the classic line from the *Pogo* comic strip: "We have met the enemy and he is us"? That's how I felt when I became an editor after a dozen years of active freelancing.

Before my work as an editor, things used to be black and white. Freelancers were the good guys. We wore white hats, did countless hours of research, endured three or four rewrites of each manuscript, and were paid an insultingly low rate per word. Editors were the bad guys. They snickered through handlebar mustaches, worked only in the afternoons, took fiendish delight in rejecting as many manuscripts as possible, and only gave freelance assignments to their friends.

Today, my perspective is different. Currently, I am a contributing editor for six national magazines. Prior to this, I worked four years as editor-in-chief of a large college alumni magazine. These experiences have almost completely reversed my points of view regarding editors and freelancers. (I've learned a lot since I knew it all.)

The truth is that an editor wears a dozen hats (none black) and is constantly being pulled in many different directions. He or she has a tremendous workload. The more you, the freelancer, can do to help an editor save time, develop ideas, secure readers, and satisfy advertisers, the more you will be helping to sell yourself and your manuscripts to that editor.

Let's take a moment to get an overview of editors' duties and see what kinds of hats they wear. Knowing these, a freelancer can lend a helping hand.

Planner

The editor must plan current and future issues of the magazine or current and future books in a publishing line, as well as help develop long-range plans for the total editorial focus of the publishing company. To assist the editor in this task, the freelancer must be alert to current news items, social trends, church developments, and reader interests. These things should be shared with editors via query letters. It's physically impossible for editors to be aware of everything new in all areas of reader interest. So, as a freelancer, you can suggest ideas and, in doing that, land assignments.

Creator

The editor is responsible for creating new projects. The book editor will be looking for writers who can predict coming trends that will make a book sell two or three years down the line. The magazine editor creates new columns, develops new series, introduces new authors, and produces fascinating layouts. Freelancers can help in the process by coming up with new styles of writing, unusual graphics such as maps, cartoons, drawings, or spectacular photos, and innovative article ideas. I once wrote *Writer's Digest* and asked if the editor would like an interview with a dead man. As I expected, no one had ever offered such an idea before. I explained that I planned to direct modern questions about writing to Jack London (who died in 1916) and then have him "respond" by quoting from passages in his novels, short stories, and articles. I received an enthusiastic go-ahead for the idea, and "Interview with Jack London" later appeared in that magazine. So, never be afraid to approach an editor with an off-the-wall idea. After all, that's what creativity is.

Copy Reader

Since most editors have few or no staff assistants, much of the proofreading, copyediting, and rewriting of manuscripts falls to the editor. A freelancer can help cut time in this process by proofreading carefully before submitting manuscripts, checking especially for spelling errors, typos, and grammatical flaws. Don't trust your word processor to know the difference between reign, rain, or rein. Similarly, if an editor sends you a galley to be checked, scrutinize it meticulously and note every error. (We will learn more about proofreading in part three of the book.)

Writer

Yes, editors are also writers. They write editorials and occasional features, and at times they fill in for an ailing or vacationing columnist—not to mention all the writing they do in responding to the "Letters to the Editor" section. They appreciate it when freelancers send them hometown editorials, thought-provoking political cartoons, workshop brochures on unique subjects, or reports that provide stimuli for new columns or editorial responses. Many times editors will reward such efforts by mentioning the freelancer in print, paying a modest finder's fee, or sending a gift subscription for the magazine to that freelancer.

Publicist

Because a magazine with low visibility is a doomed publication, editors are often involved in assisting with public relations efforts to help boost the popularity of their periodicals. Freelancers can help with this in several ways: by showing the publication to friends, relatives, and fellow writing club members; by sending a press release to a hometown newspaper whenever the freelancer has an article in a current issue of the magazine; and by requesting that local newsstands stock and display the magazine.

Scout

Like baseball managers searching for tomorrow's new home-run king, editors are always scouting for hot new writers to add to their stable of freelancers. If, after having read several back issues of a magazine, you feel you have what it takes to become a regular stringer for that publication, help the editor "discover" you by sending him or her a brief résumé and several published writing samples. Often, if editors have no current openings for new columnists or contributing editors, they will keep your materials on file for future reference or they will recommend you to another editor. In either case, you win.

Naturally, these duties are by no means the only responsibilities of an editor. These are the most crucial ones for freelancers to understand, however. Editors *do* like to help writers, and they *do* like to find quality manuscripts. If, as a freelancer, you can lend a helping hand to the editors you wish to work with, you will not only make several manuscript sales, you will also win a friend or two. As your writing career advances, you will want to come back to this section to remind yourself of the ways you can enhance your working relationship with magazine, newspaper, and book editors.

QUALITY CONTROL

Already in this section we have seen that quality research and quality writing are the two things editors value most. That is important to you as a developing writer. But do you know how to ensure that the research and writing you do will carry a stamp of quality? Maybe you have never given it any thought. You should.

Many writers have the misconception that quality control relates only to manufactured products and not to services. When we think of quality control, we usually envision someone sitting next to a conveyor belt pulling off parts that have cracks or nicks in them. We seldom relate quality control to service occupations such as drafting novels, writing speeches, and researching magazine articles and books.

These conceptions are wrong, however. In both manufacturing and services, quality control means just one thing: *doing each portion of the job exactly right the first time.* The simple fact is, flawless work saves you time, money, and grief. Consider three simple examples of how a lack of quality control in the writing business can make things go awry.

You set up an appointment to discuss the outline of your novel with a publisher. As the two of you sit down to go over the outline, you discover that *somehow* two pages have been left out. The publisher frowns and looks impatient. He begins to drum his fingers. You smile weakly, clear your throat, and ask for a new appointment. The publisher says, "Sure. But let me call you. Really, I need some more time to think about this."

It's raining one morning for the first time in two weeks. You dig out your raincoat, put it on, and find a note to yourself in one of the pockets. It reminds you to return a call to one of your sources at city hall. You slap your forehead, race to the phone, and make the call. Your source tells you that she had seen a copy of the new city budget three days before it was released. She wanted to tell you the highlights. When you didn't call back, she gave the information to another freelance reporter.

You finally land that big book contract. You are so excited about it, you make a typographical error when filling out the royalty payment forms for the publisher's accounting department. Six months later your first royalty check is sent to 1219 Mark Avenue instead of 1219 Park Avenue. Your check is delayed two weeks while the post office and publisher try to track you down.

No doubt you can add to this list your own horror stories about misspellings, inaccurate statistics, misquoted sources, missed deadlines, dried ink pens, forgotten spare film, dead tape recorder batteries, and forgotten interview appointments. In each instance it always seems to be a small matter, such as a misplaced paper, a forgotten note, or a minor typing error, that causes a great deal of confusion and trouble. These things continue to happen when writers lack a *quality* system that *controls* all variables in the business aspects of their writing.

Researchers have discovered that most mistakes are caused by a lack of attention rather than a lack of knowledge. The fault does not lie in one's training, facilities, equipment, or environment (after all, a lack of knowledge can be overcome by study). A lack of attention, however, is another problem. As Shakespeare wrote in *Julius Caesar*, "The fault, dear Brutus, is not in our stars, but in ourselves."

We have grown up being told that "to err is human, to forgive divine!" This is nonsense when it comes to professional standards. What we as writers should be saying is that "to err is inhumane, to forgive, inappropriate." If we focus on doing things once and doing them right, we won't have to worry about erring. We need to be cognizant of the fact that human error can cause the complete reworking of a manuscript, the dissatisfaction of an editor, or the failure of a book's sales campaign. These are headaches none of us need.

We could take a lesson or two from big business. Manufacturing companies realized twenty years ago that a double standard existed between employers and workers. The workers wanted the companies to allow them a 10 percent margin of error on their work. After all, they argued, nobody is perfect. This margin of error was one-sided, however. If the company made any errors on pay vouchers, vacation days, or benefits, the workers immediately filed a union grievance. They wanted to be forgiven for a certain portion of their "unavoidable" mistakes, but they wanted the employer to do everything perfectly.

Company executives restudied this concept of error margin and found it to be inappropriate. In what other profession was error acceptable? Were physicians allowed to kill 10 percent of their patients? Were parachute packers allowed to mess up one parachute in ten? Were wrecking crews forgiven if they got the address wrong only once in ten jobs?

Of course, the answer was always no. And upon realizing this, many major manufacturers initiated a zero-defects operational plan for their workers. It took some time to develop, but once functional, it resulted in saving millions of dollars and hundreds of workhours.

As a professional writer, you need to bring the same meticulous zero-defects planning to your operational procedures. You don't want to *detect* errors; you want to *prevent* them altogether. Do not accept errors as part of your writing business. If your research and writing prove to be unreliable, you will never sell to the same editor twice. If, on the other hand, you demonstrate yourself to be a reliable writer the editor knows can be trusted, you will reach that goal of getting repeat sales and assignments.

BECOMING QUALITY ORIENTED

To establish a game plan for initiating quality control into our writing careers, we need first to see what causes quality to slip and then to see how that slipping can be stopped. Experts generally cite five reasons for a lack of quality control in service occupations such as ours. They include: lack of attention, lack of desire, a poor attitude, a refusal to accept instruction, and a lack in understanding the necessity of being more alert and careful.

A lack of attention occurs when freelance writers begin to take things for granted. They don't check to make sure that all the pages of a book proposal are in place because they always have been before. They don't check their facts and spell a name wrong or attribute an act to the wrong person because their memory was always correct before this. They don't double-check the typing on important contracts because it has always been accurate before. Then the day comes when the writer takes too much for granted, and it costs a manuscript sale or worse. In all matters, freelancers must be ever vigilant for error prevention.

A lack of desire can be brought on by physical illness, temporary mental stress, a dull routine, or a lack of personal incentives. When this occurs it is better to call a "time out" (a vacation, some prayer time, a few days off, a walk in the country) rather than to force oneself to press on. Poor quality will be the result of writing at that point.

A poor attitude is a personal matter. However, each writer should remember that a good attitude toward defect prevention is all that stands between mediocrity and a great performance. Quality control is not motivation, but motivation is needed to initiate and maintain quality control.

Refusing to accept instruction always leads to weakened quality control. Writers must gain time in the advancement of their careers by learning from the wisdom of others. They must be eager to attend writing conferences, to read new books and new articles that contain ideas to improve writing, and to listen to the advice and counsel of more experienced writers and editors. The quality of one's research, writing style, and manuscript selling can always be improved if a writer can just find the right person to show him or her a new way or different approach. A writer must not only be willing to accept such instruction when it comes his or her way, but also be out diligently seeking it.

A lack in understanding actually may be something a writer is *unknowingly* guilty of. With the reading of this book, however, the scales will be falling from your eyes. Now aware, it's up to you to implement this awareness into a program that makes you careful and maintains your alertness.

In making a plan of attack for developing quality control in your writing and manuscript marketing, begin by asking yourself these three basic questions:

1. What are my most troublesome areas?
2. What are my most expensive areas for research and manuscript preparation?
3. Which of my goals are unreasonable or unnecessary?

In answering the first question you may develop a list of such factors as poor time management, careless typing, bad grammar, or, for the more advanced writer, an unsteady manuscript sales record. By listing these problems, you can then make a list of possible solutions. Any step toward overcoming troublesome areas is a step toward quality control.

In noting your greatest writing expenses (question number two), you may list such things as computer repairs, high on-line service fees, and payment for poor-quality photographic development. To lower these high costs, you will need to instill a need for quality control in everyone you work with, from the secretary who types your final drafts (which could be *you*) to the person who does maintenance work on your computer; from the printer who prepares your business cards to the processor who develops your photographs. Strict quality control in all matters results in saved time and money.

In analyzing your goals (question number three), you need to focus on where you are in your writing career *today*. It is great to set high goals for yourself and to have ambition, but just as you cannot set the cart before the horse, you likewise cannot win the National Book Award before you publish a book. A writer in the first year or two of freelancing should not set goals so unattainable that they begin to cause frustration and panic. If you run yourself ragged trying to accomplish an unreasonable task, you will wind up doing most jobs halfway. You will compromise your integrity as a trustworthy researcher and writer, and you will damage your professional reputation. Once that happens, your career will lose all its quality. Develop systems and processes that are foolproof, and build your writing career solidly on a quality base.

Philip Crosby, the famed zero-defects man at ITT, once stated, "Quality is free. What costs money are the unquality things—all the actions that involve not doing the job right the first time."

Theoretically, Crosby was right in regard to saved time and overall expenses. In practice, however, he exaggerated the circumstances. Actually, quality is not free. It costs a *lot* of money to buy better machines (the most current software, a reliable on-line server) and better materials (24-pound bond typing paper) and to hire better trained assistants (typists, photographers, researchers, book doctors). Still, when compared to the costs of lost rapport with an editor or missed assignments or libel suits for slander or lost royalty payments, the costs of quality control are minimal.

So, write correctly. It's worth the effort.

Having once produced a quality manuscript, you will next need to market it. Part four of this book will take you step by step through that procedure, so I won't discuss that now. However, one thing we *do* need to discuss now is your relationship to the money you will be earning as a writer. Cash flow is an important element in the life of a writer, and it is the biggest issue that keeps people from doing the writing they love. Because of that, you need to gain a proper perspective on how to manage your writing income. The next chapter focuses on that topic.

CHAPTER TWO

Cash, Copyrights, and Clocks

No matter where you are on the writing continuum—a beginning writer with only one piece published or an experienced writer ready to work at it full time—you will need to consider the basics of time and money management to achieve your goals. Although I am not advocating that you quit your day job and jump into a full-time writing career, that may be a reasonable long-term goal. But that's not what this chapter is about.

This chapter will instead help you take the first steps in setting up shop as a writer. You'll learn how to make time for writing, how to understand the rules and nature of the work, and even how to comprehend the laws related to it. Once you know what all is involved, the next logical step (explained in subsequent chapters) will be to learn how to do the actual writing.

During an interview some years ago, I asked singer Johnny Cash, "Is it true you used to make a living by picking cotton?"

Cash scowled. "I made an *existence* picking cotton," he corrected me. "No one makes a *living* picking cotton."

I sometimes feel that same way when people look at me with amazement and say, "Wow! You make your living entirely from freelance writing, eh?"

Depending on how a career and its cash flow are going at the time that question is given, any freelance writer could give a variety of responses. At certain times of the year, such as royalty statement day, a writer is flush with funds. At other times, he or she may be making only an "existence."

Overall, however, I have survived rather well since turning to freelance writing full time many years ago. And, through trial and error (read: "fail and terror"), I have become more efficient each year at money management. In this chapter, I will offer my guidelines to help you live more comfortably on the money you earn as a writer, particularly if your goal is to depend substantially on your writing income for sustenance. Then, I will discuss copyright issues. And third, I will provide a number of time management tips to help you find the time you need to write.

MONEY MANAGEMENT

Determine Your Financial Role as a Writer

Are you just writing for the enjoyment you gain from sharing your views with others, or are you planning to do it as the sole source of support for your family? Is writing just something you do for a little extra cash, or is it a true second income? You cannot set a cash goal until you determine how many cash obligations you have.

Evaluate Your Hourly Rate

Add up the total amount of cash you received for your first three periodical sales and divide that total by the number of hours it took you to research, write, type, and submit all that material. This will tell you how much you made per hour. It might also be helpful to ask other writers in the field, such as members of a writing club, what they are getting paid by various publishers so that you can develop a standard rate. If someone wants an article or wants to hire you to write something, you then will know what to charge.

Prepare a Budget

Make two lists. One will be a list of the obvious costs you are required to cover in order to stay in business as a writer (on-line monthly service fees, paper, stamps, computer maintenance and updates, travel expenses, conference costs, phone calls). The other list will outline the household expenses you are required to meet (food, rent, clothing, utilities, or the portion of these that you want covered, if any, by your writing income). These lists will give you a clear picture of what your total cash flow needs are per month.

Set Up Three Business Books

An informal system will work for you at first; a more formal one will be needed as your writing takes on greater economic importance.

First, you will need a *checkbook* so that all of your expenses will be legitimately documented by canceled checks should you ever be audited by the Internal Revenue Service. Of course, at the beginning you can use your personal checking account. Once your sales volume increases you will want a separate business account.

Second, you will also need a *journal* so that you can record the date, payee, cash amount, item purchased, and check number for all expenses related to your writing.

Finally, you will need a *cash receipts journal* to record all your freelance sales and royalty payments. Be sure to note the date the check was issued, its payer, the amount, the check number, and for what manuscript the money was paid. (Your tax on this income can be paid quarterly.)

Establish a Guaranteed Monthly Positive Cash Flow

Cash flow for freelance articles will be sporadic and unpredictable, but monthly bills will be constant and inflexible. You need to secure some kind of work that will guarantee a set amount of income each month, especially if you eventually turn to writing full time. Perhaps you can teach a continuing education class at a local college's night school or write a column for a newspaper or magazine or run a part-time résumé service. You might even want to do what I've done: invest some of your royalty earnings in rental real estate that generates monthly rent payments while also providing a tax depreciation credit. Do whatever you feel most comfortable doing, but *never jump into freelance writing full time without some guarantee of regular, adequate cash flow from some source.*

Develop Some Long-Term Income-Producing Projects

Instead of churning out one article after another in a frenzied attempt to generate immediate cash flow, allot some of your weekly writing time to writing books. Once a book is written and published it may earn money for you even when you are sleeping, eating lunch, or taking a vacation. This is called passive income. You no longer have to do the work, yet the earnings continue. This takes a lot of pressure off you in regard to feeling you have to be pounding the keyboard around the clock. However, writing a book does not guarantee such income. Many times a book will barely pay off its advance (the money you received and probably spent during the writing process) before going out of print. But if it does begin selling steadily, it can provide regular income.

Capitalize on Tax Deductions

Have your accountant determine the best way to handle expenses. You may wish to amortize the depreciation of your computer, tape recorder, camera, and other new equipment over five years so that you will always have sizable yearly tax write-offs. Or, if you receive a large lump sum payment, buy yourself a computer or some new office furniture or file cabinets, and use accelerated depreciation to reduce your present tax bite, should that continue to be an option allowed by the IRS.

Pay Yourself a Set Weekly or Monthly Salary

Today most families depend on two income earners. By paying yourself a regular salary, whether you are the primary breadwinner or not, your family will know how much your regular financial contributions will be. This will keep your household on an even keel. Be sure to set aside money each month for taxes, and try to invest 5 percent of whatever you earn (net), even if it only allows you to buy one savings bond or contribute to one mutual fund per month. In time, you will build an emergency contingency fund.

Diversify Your Writing Talents at Every Opportunity

As noted earlier, the more you are qualified to do, the more you will be able to do. So, learn how to write fiction, nonfiction, business articles, interviews, religious materials, poetry, audio scripts, children's literature, and screenplays. Get the word out to editors that if something needs to be written, you are the person who can write it.

Behave Like a Businessperson

Always be developing new assignments so that you can keep yourself supplied with work. Go for the easy money first (reprints, excerpt sales, audio/screen rights) on things you've already done. Never, never, never depend on one market to support you. Don't live on advances (that's mortgaging your future), but do get the largest possible advance from publishers for your book projects. Be willing to assist publishers in promoting your writings, particularly your books. Don't be afraid to ask for reimbursements on the expenses you incur while doing legwork research for freelance articles.

Writing for money and managing money are two completely different things. In order to be free to do the former, a freelancer must be adept at the latter. That requires a plan such as the one I have just explained.

Having once made money as a writer, you will next need to know how to report your earnings and expenses to the Internal Revenue Service.

PAYING TAXES

They say the only two sure things in life are death and taxes. I pray you have prepared for the former; let's now discuss how to deal with the latter.

The key word to remember when dealing with the Internal Revenue Service is *documentation*. If you are going to deduct something as a legitimate business expense, you are going to have to prove you spent the money. So, rule one is this: Pay by credit card or check, or get a receipt.

What are "legitimate expenses" related to a career in freelance writing? Actually, there are many, and I have noted some of them here.

Consultation expenses. If you hire an editor to proofread and edit your manuscript before submitting it to a publisher, that expense is deductible. So is the tax preparation fee your accountant charges you.

Professional journals. The writing magazines, newsletters, trade journals, and writing annuals you subscribe to are deductible expenses. So are the costs of a few training books each year (such as the one you are now reading).

Business calls. Calls to your editors, publishers, literary agent, accountant, and to people you use as interview sources for your articles or books are all deductible. Keep a record of everyone you call, when and why you made the call, its results, and its cost.

Supplies. Paper and ink cartridges for your printer, correction fluid, pencils, ink pens, notepads, film, cassette tapes, business letterhead, envelopes, and other expendable items needed to maintain a writing career are deductible expenses.

Postage. All costs related to mailing query letters, manuscripts, and business bills may be deducted. If you don't use metered mail, you can ask for receipts from the postal workers from whom you make purchases. If you don't submit material by electronic transfer, then also deduct the cost of envelopes.

Safe deposit box. If you rent a safe deposit box to store valuable interview tapes, original manuscripts, or rare photographs, you may deduct the cost of the box. If you use half the box for personal items (deeds, bonds, jewelry) and half for your writing materials, only 50 percent of the cost of the box may be deducted.

Equipment and furnishings. The equipment related to a career in writing, such as a computer and printer, a desk, a photocopier, a cassette tape recorder, or a camera, qualifies for both tax investment credits and tax write-offs. Often your accountant will amortize the cost of these items over five or ten years.

Business mileage. A set amount per mile may be deducted whenever you use your car to drive to interviews, writers' conferences, meetings with editors or publishers, and for trips to TV appearances or book autograph parties for promotional purposes. An efficient way to keep track of your mileage is to record the date, your destination, and the beginning and ending odometer readings in a journal designated specifically for this purpose and kept in your car.

Self-improvement courses. Tuition costs for writing classes and writers' conferences and seminars are usually deductible if the writing is not merely a hobby.

Passport. If you travel for book research or as a travel writer for a newspaper or magazine, the costs of your passport and visa are deductible.

Interest fees. Anytime you pay interest on a home mortgage, that interest is deductible on income taxes. Sometimes writers who don't yet have much writing income offset their expenses by taking out a second mortgage (home equity loan) to purchase computers or office equipment. Mortgage interest on a second mortgage may also be tax deductible. Check with your accountant.

Home office. If you maintain an office in your home that is used strictly for your writing, you may be able to deduct that part of your rent or mortgage payment from your taxes. For example, if you have nine rooms in your home and one is an office, you may deduct one-ninth of your rent or mortgage payments as a business expense. The same rule applies to your heating and electric bills each month. In recent years the IRS has allowed partial home office deductions, as well. For example, if half of your family room is set up as an office, you can still take a portion of your household expenses as a deduction. The stickler on this latter condition, however, is that the IRS often wants proof that the expenses are offsetting some legitimate profit from your writing. Be sure to check with an accountant on this.

As I explained earlier, in addition to your checkbook, you will need to maintain two sets of business books. Your first will be a cash receipts journal. This is a record of all receipts, including checks. It records payments received (royalties, advances, expense allowances, work-for-hire paychecks, and so on), including payments on account. Your setup should include columns for the *date* the payment arrived, the *payer* (magazine's name or book company's name), the *check number,* the *amount,* and a *running total.*

You will also need a cash disbursements journal which will list all of your writing-related expenses. The setup should include columns for the *date* the expense was incurred, the *receiver* of the payment, your *check number* (or receipt record), the *amount* paid out, the *item purchased,* and a *running total* of the year's expenses.

Once your business grows, you may want to keep your books on computer using one of the accounting programs for lay people. While initially taking a good deal of time to learn, this can be a time saver if you have a large volume of expenses and income.

Keep in mind that tax laws are anything but constant. Because of inevitable changes to the tax code, be sure to have a qualified accountant assist you in your tax work each year. You can help your own cause a great deal, however, by starting now to institute the above tips.

UNDERSTANDING COPYRIGHTS

As long as we are discussing IRS rulings and requirements, we may as well look at another branch of the federal government that also has an impact on authors: the Copyright Office.

Entire books have been written to explain how United States copyrights work. The Library of Congress itself has published forty-seven different booklets on the subject (thirty-one of which may be obtained free of charge). For our purposes, however, let's just touch upon what you need to know in order to get your career started. Let's begin by defining key terms.

Work-for-Hire

The phrase *work-for-hire* implies that an author has been guaranteed a set payment for a project during specific period of time, and the person paying the author becomes the legal owner of the project that the author writes during that time period. For example, if someone offers to pay you $725 per week to work as a newspaper reporter for one year, then everything you write during that year belongs to the newspaper that is paying your salary. In effect, you are completely out of the freelance market. On the other hand, in the book and magazine industries, only the work done on a particular project is a work-for-hire. You could conceivably be working on several projects at once and perhaps only one is a work-for-hire.

The importance to you of the work-for-hire law is that as a freelancer you will *not* own the writing you have been hired to do. The rights to the finished manuscript will be held by the publisher who hired you to write it. You will be paid a one-time fee. You will not collect royalties, reprint earnings, or any other monies earned by the finished manuscript. Furthermore, you may not slightly modify your material and then try to market it as a new and separate work.

All Rights

The term *all rights offered* means that the author is selling complete ownership of a finished manuscript to a periodical or book publisher. The author will receive one payment for the manuscript. After that, the author may not resell that manuscript in any form or make any claim of ownership regarding it. Conversely, the newspaper or magazine buying all rights to the manuscript may print the material whenever, wherever, and as many times as it wishes without paying further for it. Here's an example of all rights offered: You write an article on how to prepare a job résumé, and a magazine pays you $575 for all rights to that article. Later, the magazine may run the article twice in the same year, but you will receive no extra money for the later appearances of the article. You don't own that article any longer. Even if the magazine chooses to run your article as a chapter in a book on job hunting, you would receive no royalties from the sale of that book. You waived all future rights to that article when you accepted the $575 and agreed to sell all rights. About one in five contemporary magazines insists on retaining all rights, so be careful what you agree to sell.

One-Time Rights

Another term you may hear occasionally is *first North American serial rights only.* Prior to the revision of the U.S. Copyright Law in 1976 and 1978, this phrase would be typed on an author's manuscript if the author were selling one-time rights to a North American publisher. In other words, the publisher would purchase the manuscript and have complete ownership of it until it appeared in print. However, once the work appeared in a newspaper or magazine, the ownership of that manuscript immediately reverted to the author, who was then free to sell it again somewhere else.

Under this old system many authors would go through all of the formal procedures of filling in Copyright Form TX, paying a copyright registration fee, and submitting to the Copyright Office a sample copy of the original manuscript being copyrighted. Since January 1, 1978, this is no longer necessary, although it still may be done if an author wishes to follow the full procedure.

Your Copyright

Today, in order to hold the copyright to your material, all you need to do is type on your manuscript the word *Copyright,* the year of completion, and the name of the owner of the copyright (you). The word *Copyright* may be abbreviated as *Copr.* or as ©. Here is how it should appear:

> Copyright 2004 by Dennis E. Hensley; or
> Copr. 2004 by Dennis E. Hensley; or
> © 2004 by Dennis E. Hensley.

Putting any one of these three notices at the top of the first page of your manuscript (see part four of this book for manuscript preparation information) offers the same protection today that "First North American Serial Rights Only" offered prior to 1978. You no longer have to pay the registration fee or file Form TX with the Copyright Office. And, this can be used to protect book manuscripts as well as articles.

As I've noted elsewhere in this book, some authors don't put the copyright symbol on their manuscripts any longer because they feel that all current editors understand the rules of the natural copyright law. But, as I have also said, some writers (myself included) still like to proclaim boldly at the top of each new manuscript who the owner is. In my case, I've had six out-of-court settlements with publishers who have accidentally violated my copyright by printing something of mine in book form. With this in mind, I am a fanatic about doing all I can to establish ownership of what I write.

When negotiating a book contract, the copyright can reside with the author or with the publisher or can be co-owned by both depending on the terms of the contract. Up until the point at which you sign such a contract, however, you own the rights.

If you have any questions regarding copyright procedures, there are several ways you can obtain free assistance. First, you may write to the Registrar of Copyrights, c/o the U.S. Library of Congress, Washington, D.C. 20559, and ask to be sent these free-of-charge pamphlets: Circular R99, "Highlights of the New Copyright Law," and Circular R1-d, "New Copyright Registration Procedures." Second, you may telephone the Copyright Office at (202) 287-8700 and ask to speak with an information specialist. You will have to pay for the phone call, but the consultation will be free. Third, you may send your written questions to the Copyright Information Center, Suite 480, 1707 L Street NW, Washington, D.C. 20559. Fourth, you are also free to write to your congressional representative and have him or her send you a copy of Public Law 94-553, dated October 19, 1976. You then can sit down and read the entire copyright law for yourself. And fifth, you can visit the Copyright Information pages, part of the Library of Congress Web site, at *http://lcweb.loc.gov/copyright/*.

Fair Use
One final term you need to understand in regard to copyright is *fair use*. Under the new copyright law, you may use a portion of a copyrighted prose work

without asking the author's (or his or her publisher's) permission and without paying the author if you use the work for research, scholarship, criticism, commentary, teaching, or news reporting. All you need to do is properly cite the source, including author, publication, date, and page. Note, however, that lines of poetry and song lyrics do not fall under this fair use practice.

Despite the freedom of this new law, many writers feel that ethics and courtesy still dictate that authors and/or publishers should be contacted for granting permission before any substantial portion of an author's work is used by another writer. Here are some further guidelines for understanding the difference between fair use and copyright violation.

You will be in violation of copyright if you use another person's written material for your personal gain or if you fail to give proper credit to the original writer. In determining whether use of material falls within the realm of fair use, judges look at these four points:

1. The nature of the copyrighted work;
2. The amount and substantiality of the portion used in relationship to the copyrighted work as a whole;
3. The effect of the use upon the potential market for or value of the copyrighted work (meaning that quoting a portion of a work for a book review would be of value to the person being quoted and so would be fair, but taking a large section of her article or book to supplement your own article or book would be unfair); and
4. The purpose and character of the use, including whether such use is of a commercial nature (meaning that the writer or publisher will make a profit from the use of that excerpt) or is for nonprofit educational purposes.

When it comes to using another author's work as part of your current project, you will usually be safe if you follow the golden rule. If you're a published writer, you know how it feels when people misuse your material—either they use too much of it or perhaps they misquote you or don't use the material in a positive light. If you're not a published writer, you soon will be. How will *you* wish to be treated?

Two books are worth reading regarding the fair use clause of the Copyright

Law: *The Rights of Authors and Artists* by Kenneth Norwick and Jerry Crasen (Bantam, 1985) and *Law and the Writer* by Kirk Polking (Writer's Digest Books, 1985).

FINDING TIME TO WRITE

You have had a lot of material thrown at you in this first section. By now you may be wondering whether or not a career in writing is worth all this effort. Don't despair; it *is* worth it. The exhilaration you will feel when you see your byline in print will quickly erase any memories of struggles you faced in getting to that point.

Besides, there has never been a more opportune time to enter the field of freelance writing. At the start of the twenty-first century there are more than seven thousand secular and religious newspapers, magazines, and book publishers actively seeking freelance material, both in hard copy form and for online use. Some periodicals, such as *Reader's Digest,* are paying as much as $5,000 per accepted freelance manuscript. Others pay only a few cents per word but offer great opportunities for new writers to break into the field.

But why, you may wonder, would an editor be eager to use anything you might write? Why would publishers pay ten dollars or even thousands of dollars for your individual freelance articles? There are several answers to those questions.

To begin with, freelance writers save editors and publishers a lot of money. Unlike a staff writer, who must be paid a salary and also be given insurance coverage, a dental plan, a retirement plan, worker's compensation, vacations with pay, a private office, and Social Security coverage, the freelancer receives just the negotiated payment for the accepted manuscript. This allows the publisher to reduce overhead costs drastically.

Freelance articles prevent a magazine from becoming mono-toned. If every article is written in-house, the periodical develops a stylistic redundancy that bores readers. The insertion of articles by outside writers adds a refreshing change of pace to the overall content and voice, which appeals to readers.

Freelancers give breadth and depth. By having a geographically widespread string of freelancers, an editor can be based in Manhattan or Fort Wayne or Nashville or Los Angeles and still be able to receive "on the spot" news coverage from across the country. This gives a depth of information to a periodical.

Freelancers save on staff time. A freelancer may be willing to spend three or four weeks preparing a feature that otherwise might not get written because a regular staffer couldn't be "lost" from the office for that long.

So, as you can surmise, the contribution you as a freelancer can make is of tremendous value to editors. They are willing to make it of value to you, too. And that is why the time spent in developing your writing career is time well spent.

But just where are you going to get the needed time to do your writing and manuscript marketing? You may be telling yourself that your schedule is already so crammed there is no way you can find time to enhance your status as a writer. Ah, but that's where you are wrong. I believe that if you use only two hours per day, Monday through Friday, you could develop into a working professional writer within one year without interrupting anything in your already established routine.

Let's suppose that you work an eight-hour day and that you sleep eight hours each night. That still leaves you with eight hours of discretionary time each twenty-four-hour period. Let's imagine that during six of those remaining eight hours you spend time getting ready for work, traveling to your job or running errands, watching television, preparing and eating meals, talking on the phone, caring for family, and doing anything else that strikes your fancy. Two of those eight hours you can safeguard each day to devote to writing.

It will not matter which two-hour period you prefer to use for writing. Some writers prefer 6:00 to 8:00 A.M. before leaving for work; others prefer noon until 2:00 P.M. while the children are down for a nap or are playing quietly. As for me, when I first started, I wrote from 9:00 to 11:00 P.M. when things got quiet at night. (When you first start writing you may need to try for half-hour segments snatched a few times per day and then build up as you go along. For example, at-home moms with active children probably won't be able to work a full two hours until they've made some manuscript sales and can justify hiring a sitter to give them blocks of freedom.)

The result is the same. At the end of the first week, you will have logged ten hours of writing. At the end of the first month, you will have logged the equivalent of a forty-hour week of writing. At the end of one year, you will have logged the equivalent of three full months of writing. And the amazing part of all this is that you have still been able to sleep eight hours a day, hold down a job, and keep your weekends free. So, you see, if you truly have a desire to be a writer, there are enough hours in the day to get the job done.

There are some ways you can help yourself find additional time for writing in your busy schedule. I offer these time management tips.

- *Learn to say no to people without feeling guilty.* Take a little time to enhance the talents you've been blessed with. Don't try to take on every job and responsibility offered to you.
- *Abandon the daylong open-door policy.* When it's time to write, go to your writing area, seclude yourself, and guard your privacy. Explain kindly but unmistakably to family members and friends that you cannot be interrupted. If you're married and have small children, work out an arrangement with your spouse so that you can take turns being with the children while you each have some private time.
- *Control your work environment.* If the decor distracts you, change it. If there is foot traffic in the hall, close the door. If there is noise outside, use the drone of a dehumidifier or an FM radio station played low as background "white" noise.
- *Assemble all of your supplies in advance.* Don't bob up and down out of your chair to get a pencil or a pair of scissors or a cup of coffee. Sit and work. Apply the seat of your pants to the seat of your chair and produce words.
- *Plan a work pause of five minutes each half-hour* rather than long coffee breaks. This time will refresh you, yet you will not have to reorient yourself completely to the manuscript you were working on.
- *Set self-imposed deadlines* on your projects and adhere to these schedules in your writing regimen.

Before long you will discover that daily writing can become as routine as daily devotions, prayer time, family activity time, or anything else you have scheduled into a regular day. As each week passes, you will not only increase your writing skills, you will also increase the number of freelance manuscripts you will have in the mail. That is when you will have become a professional freelance writer.

Having read this far, your view of freelance writing may be completely different than what you had previously imagined. That's all right. That's growth. Part of the maturing process in becoming a writer is learning to separate fantasies from reality. This book will deal only in reality.

That is not to say, however, that the joys and rewards associated with writing won't often seem fantastic. In truth, this is a buoyant and thrilling occupation. I've had many jobs in my life—teacher, soldier, musician, public orator—but nothing has ever equaled the sustained excitement I have had over my career as a writer.

I know that you can identify with this; if not, you never would have been compelled to read this book.

In the next section, we will discuss methods and procedures for finding dozens upon dozens of ideas to write about.

PART II

What to Write About

Ideas for articles, stories, and books are the mainstay of any writer's career. Most writers have something special in mind for that first big writing quest; after that, however, they often feel as though their reservoir of ideas has dried up.

A missionary once told me, "I wrote a long article about my years in Brazil, and the article was accepted for publication. I was ecstatic until I remembered that I still wanted to be a writer, but now I knew of nothing else to write about."

Another person, a housewife, told me, "I had an idea for making family discussions more fun at dinnertime. I sold it to a women's magazine. Two weeks later the editor sent me a letter asking for more articles. I panicked. I had no idea how working writers came up with new topics and subjects to write about."

If you have ever found yourself in a similar situation, let me put your mind at rest. The fact is, there are so many things to write about, you will never live long enough to tap even 10 percent of what is available to you.

In this section I will review the standard article topics editors *always* need, and I will provide advice about how to research them and write about them. I will also show how you, as a writer, can predict news trends as much as six months in advance. Not only that, but you'll learn how to use such common everyday items as an almanac or a newspaper to discover feature ideas and even story plots. Finally, I will review ways in which your own life story might be the right topic for you to write about next.

Most of this information is geared toward writing articles, in part because that is the bread and butter of the freelance writer who is making a living at it. But there are plenty of lessons here for those interested in books.

CHAPTER THREE

Finding a Salable Subject

Let's begin by looking at the ten most dependable article ideas that sales-oriented writers know editors want.

TEN STANDARD TOPICS

In order to sell magazines, editors have to offer articles that readers will be eager to read. Certain subjects are recurring favorites with readers, and if you are aware of them, you will find ready markets for your material.

Money

Readers are fascinated by articles that explain new ways to save, spend, make, and use money. If you have an innovative approach to establishing an IRA, saving grocery coupons or reducing taxes, you will find a market for your article in both religious and secular publications. Topics such as effective fundraising techniques for Christian day schools or contemporary views of the Old Testament tradition of tithing are of specialized value to religious markets.

Physical Fitness

Editors are constantly looking for articles on new diets, innovative exercise programs, ways to live longer, and tips for looking better. In recent years articles have appeared on how to do aerobic workouts to country music, how to exercise the body and mind simultaneously by memorizing poetry while weightlifting, and how to use sports programs to draw youngsters to vacation Bible schools.

How-to Features

Readers frequently buy magazines because they contain articles that teach such things as how to fix a chair, buy a car, apply for a job, or plan a vacation. The standard how-to article is always a popular feature. If you know how to teach people how to do something in a faster, cheaper, or better way, get it down on paper and send it to an editor.

Mental Health

People in today's society are being confronted with a multitude of problems in the areas of unemployment, inflation, computerization, race relations, population control, and family disintegration. These often lead to mental and emotional struggles. Editors are seeking articles on such topics as overcoming stress, handling burnout, and dealing with personal acceptance problems. Interviews with psychologists and psychiatrists on these and related topics will find ready markets. Articles on more specialized topics, such as pastoral fatigue, the alienation of teenagers, and marital conflict, are always needed by religious publications. By narrowing the focus on a broad topic, you can develop an idea into one that an editor will buy.

Lifestyles

People are intrigued by the way other people live and work and socialize. How does a monk exist in solitude? What does a king eat for breakfast? What is it like to be a traveling salesperson who lives out of a suitcase forty-five weeks per year? What sort of daily regimen does a translator in Iraq have? These and similar questions are answered in lifestyle features about both common and uncommon people. Editors are always on the lookout for captivating features about people with unusual lifestyles.

Profiles

Not only do readers want to know about lifestyles, they also want to know about people themselves, particularly famous or unusual people. In my years as a journalist, I have had the chance to interview many celebrities, from Canadian novelist Janette Oke to former United Nations Ambassador Andrew Young. Naturally, features on such people are easy to sell. But equally easy to sell are articles on unusual people. I have sold articles about a man who invented a two-wheel car, a man who collected fifty-four thousand specimens of moths, a woman who created quilt designs, a boy who became a black-smith with a mobilized livery stable, and a retiree who became an actor at age sixty-eight. Their unusual stories and unique personalities made very readable copy.

Though many of these ideas are for magazines, always keep the book idea in mind. If you're a nonfiction writer, personality profiles can also add action, drama, and plot tension to your nonfiction books. When I wrote a book on the forty-year history of the organization Youth for Christ, I filled the book with profiles of Billy Graham, Torrey Johnson, George Beverly Shea, Ted Engstrom, and other great leaders who had achieved amazing things during their years with the organization. These profiles gave a sense of human triumph and made the book lively and interesting.

Activities

With the advent of many of our modern timesaving devices, many people are finding themselves with time on their hands. They often turn to magazines for ways to fill their time. They are seeking ideas for individual activities (crafts, projects), family activities (games, outings, celebrations), or group activities (parties, trips, programs, seminars, workshops). If you have such ideas, you will find editors eager to see them.

Self-Help

Readers are always looking for feature articles that can show them ways to advance themselves. Articles on how to dress for success, improve one's grammar, enhance one's public image, or develop a more positive outlook on life are always of interest to editors. In the Christian market, in particular, readers need articles on how to teach Sunday school more dynamically, how to memorize Scripture more readily, how to witness more effectively, and how to serve one another more empathetically.

Amusement

People frequently discover interesting places to go, things to see, and people to watch by reading feature articles about these topics in magazines. If you have an idea for an entertainment-related feature, no doubt you will find a market for it. Make it newsy, fill it with specifics related to costs, dates, and reservations, and give a general overview of the entertainment aspects of the topic.

Education

Parents, students, teachers, seminar leaders, and a host of other people with a connection to teaching are interested in reading about new ways to educate students of all ages. If you can write about using virtual reality in the classroom or learning subconsciously while sleeping, you will have editors eager to see your manuscripts. Anything new and exciting about the educational process is of interest to editors and readers.

These ten generic topics will give you an overview of what editors are looking for in article subjects. Obviously, these are not the *only* topics that make for publishable copy, and one magazine will take a certain type of article while another will be looking for something entirely different. Literally hundreds of additional subjects can be made into topics for feature stories.

IDEAS FOR FEATURES

Finding topics for features is quite easy, once you know how to go about searching for them. Here are some suggestions to assist you in your search.

Check local and area newspapers for small news items you can develop into long feature stories for different media. You will need to do additional legwork and research, but it will be worth it when the small item you read in your morning paper later becomes a cover story by you in a national magazine.

By way of example, perhaps you might see an article about a church in your town that has formed an effective committee to combat pornography in your area. If this committee's social and legal protests can be equally effective in other cities, you could write about their methods for your denominational magazine or a general Christian periodical. Or you could develop the article for a news-magazine, using a different slant.

Listen to radio and TV news broadcasts and find a national news item that you can write up from a local angle. For example, if it is announced that nerve gas causes cancer, find veterans in your hometown who came in contact with that gas during Desert Storm and interview them to see whether or not they have had reactions to it. How have your city's service clubs, hospitals, and churches assisted such individuals? How can other cities do likewise?

Ask for topics to write about. Whenever an insurance agent finishes selling you a policy, he asks for a referral to someone else. You can do the same thing. Whenever you finish interviewing someone for a feature article, just ask, "Do you have any friends, relatives, or colleagues who are involved in anything newsworthy that I might be able to write about?" Many times these contacts will give you several names of interesting people they know well.

Use the yellow pages of your telephone book to find article ideas and news sources.

- Send a postcard to all of the associations, organizations, and church groups listed and ask to be added to their mailing lists for bulletins, newsletters, and press releases. These items may give you several news tips.
- Check display ads for companies ready to celebrate their twenty-fifth or fiftieth anniversaries in business and then write profiles on them.
- Find businesses that offer unusual services, such as musket repair or home radar installation, and write about them.
- Develop new slants on routine businesses. For example, what is the most valuable possession ever transported by the local armored truck company? Do any local florists sell meat-eating plants, such as Venus's-flytraps? Are army surplus stores catering to doomsday advocates?
- Combine two topics. A report on the local egg producers and a report on local hog raisers could become "Ham and Eggs: The Breakfast Business."

Go to the library and read through the reference book *Facts on File.* It will tell you what the big news stories of previous years were. You then can do up-to-date features on those topics. Some examples might be "Remembering Millennial Fever" or "What Did We Learn from the Oklahoma City Bombing?"

An active freelance writer will never complain about not having anything to write about. He or she will always know where to go hunting for the next big story. For example, did you know that a common almanac and a current calendar can combine to help you come up with fifteen or more article ideas each month? It's true. Let me explain.

USING AN ALMANAC

A frequent question heard at writing workshops is, "How can I break into my local and regional newspapers?" The answer is to offer the newspapers coverage of something that is timely and of interest to many readers, yet is a topic that probably will not be covered by one of the newspaper's staff reporters.

At least fifteen such topics arise each month in the form of holidays and recognition days. Whereas editors never hesitate to assign staff reporters to develop articles related to Christmas or Independence Day, it usually falls to the freelancer to give coverage to Arbor Day, April Fool's Day, Flag Day, and the lesser national holidays, including many religious observances such as Good Friday.

Begin your research well in advance of the month your articles should break into print. Get out your current almanac and make a list of all the holidays that month. Using October as an example, your list would look something like this:

World Communion Sunday (6)
Child Health Day (7)
Yom Kippur (8)
Leif Ericson Day (9)
Farmer's Day (12), Florida
Pioneer's Day (12), South Dakota
Columbus Day (14)
Poetry Day (15)
Sweetest Day (17)

Alaska Day (18)
United Nations Day (24)
Reformation Sunday (27)
Armistice Day (28)
Nevada Day (31)
Youth Honor Day (31)
Halloween (31)
Reformation Day (31)

When you focus on a national day, conduct research that will answer the following questions:

- When was this day first observed? Where? Why? By whom?
- How will it be observed locally by clubs, churches, organizations, schools, and local dignitaries?
- Will it have an impact on local businesses that sell greeting cards, candy, flags, bumper stickers, and balloons?
- Will any speeches, parades, church services, twenty-one gun salutes, pumpkin-carving contests, or other events be linked to this day?
- How was this day celebrated in past eras?

Your local research should begin in the history section of your public library. Remember, too, to check back issues of your hometown newspaper (usually on disk or microfiche) to see what has already been covered about this day in previous years.

Put a lot of quotations in your feature. If it's an ethnic holiday, find those who can talk authoritatively—an elderly Irishman who can tell a story about Ireland for St. Patrick's Day or a rabbi who can explain the full significance of Hanukkah. For patriotic observances, interview the oldest veteran you can find for a Memorial Day feature or find a college American history professor who can comment on Citizenship Day (September 17) or National Freedom Day (February 1).

Your writing should be lively and to the point. For a first draft, pretend you have a two-minute radio show in which you can only read 245 words of copy; see how tightly you can write about the day on which you are focusing. For local newspapers your article should be no longer than 750 to 1200 words. As a filler item, limit your report to under 500 words.

Keep your finished drafts on a disk. Each year you can pull them out again, add a few new quotes or items of current information to the previously gathered background research, and then submit a revised article to a different newspaper in your area. Remember when writing for a newspaper to offer one-time rights only, so you can resell it elsewhere once it's been published.

There are approximately 190 national days listed in most unabridged almanacs. Additionally, the United States Department of Labor can provide you with a list of national business observances, such as Professional Secretaries' Day or National Pickle Week. There's never a shortage of observances to write about.

The almanac can also provide you with important dates, names, events, and landmarks you can organize into lists. List articles of any kind are easy to write and easy to market. If you're on the Internet, much of the information you'd find in an Almanac is also on-line.

LIST ARTICLES

Regular readers of my articles and books know that I am keen on lists. In fact, I love lists. I make use of them as much as possible. Lists are orderly, concise, easy to read, and informative. Readers can glance over them, tape them on refrigerators, mail them to friends, or save them for future reference. And since readers love lists, editors do, too. Since editors love lists, freelance writers must learn to love them.

The list article is one of the easiest to write and easiest to sell. Why? Let me explain by giving you a list of reasons.

1. **Titles are better.** Notice how the title "Summer Gardening Ideas" is improved when I change it to "Twelve Ways to Double Your Garden's Output." The first title is ambiguous. The second title promises something specific, and readers like specifics. Similarly, "Be a Good Web Page Designer" isn't as captivating as "Five Surefire Design Ideas to Improve Your Web Site."

2. **Organization is improved.** By jotting down on scrap paper all of the items you wish to mention in your list, you can rearrange them in chronological or sequential order. Instantly, your article outline is ready. Organization is a snap.

3. **Topics are endless.** There is virtually no end to the variety of
   things that can be listed. Consider holidays: "Six Ways to
   Redecorate a Union Hall," "Four Ways to Stuff a Turkey," or "Five
   Safety Tips for Nighttime Carolers." Consider people: "The Ten
   Most Influential Women in the Bayou," "Five Unusual Facts
   About Teddy Roosevelt," or "Six Hispanic Patriots of America."
   Consider places: "Montana's Ten Smallest Churches," "The Five
   Most Expensive Hotels in New York," "Seven Little-known Retreat
   Havens." If you have an almanac and a telephone book with yellow
   pages, you will never run out of list topics.
4. **Research is easy.** The reference section of your library can give you
   anything you need to get started on list research. You can also check
   current census reports; *The Book of Lists* by Wallechinsky, Wallace,
   and Wallace; government publications; Better Business Bureau fact
   sheets; and the Almanac. As we've already mentioned, much of this
   information is on-line, so you can conduct that research on your
   home computer (if you have Internet access) or, in most cases,
   schedule a time to use one of the computers at your library.

Outside research isn't always required. Some lists can be concocted out of
your head based on your own experience or imagination or observations. For
example, you could write "Ten Tips for Hiring a Baby-sitter," "Seven Ways to
Organize a PTA Fundraiser," or "Five Ways to Be a Better Joke Teller."

When writing your lists, you can make them more appealing to the eye by
putting a box around them as a sidebar or by setting off each item with a bullet
(dot), check, number, or letter. Most word-processing programs have plenty of
options for icons and typographic symbols.

As you get a few ideas for list articles, jot them down on a notepad that you
can carry with you. As new ideas come to you, add them. Ask people for their
comments and ideas, too. Just ask, "How do you overcome fear of talking to a
stranger about your business?" or "What current TV commercials annoy you
most?" After you get twenty or so ideas, select the ten best ones and write your
article.

I have found that list articles can do double duty. I can sell them first as freelance items and then later use them as sidebars for chapters of my books. For

example, I wrote an article on how to use time effectively during long layovers at airports. I called the piece, "Overcoming Terminal Problems," and it was published in the magazines *Roto, Gulfshore Life,* and *Market Builder.* It also became a small list of ten timesaving tips for travelers in my book *Staying Ahead of Time.* So, never throw a list away. It may become the foundation of your next book.

TRAVEL WRITING

Just as list articles are easy to put together, so too are travel articles. In fact, every time you take a vacation, you could be laying the groundwork for several travel articles. That is the way it usually happens with me.

My dear family—my wife, son, and daughter—knows that I'm addicted to writing. I never stop being a writer. Ever. Even on vacation. Especially on vacation. Family travel often stimulates my passion for writing.

Travel can be a real moneymaking part of a writer's life. I have seldom traveled anywhere without later writing about it. After coming home from service in Vietnam, I took a vacation in the Smoky Mountains with my wife. I later co-authored a Christian romance novel about a POW in Vietnam and his long-lost sister who was living in the Smoky Mountains. I drew upon firsthand experience in describing both settings.

Another time my family and I took a four-day trip to the upper peninsula of Michigan. That led to two major travel features in the *Detroit Free Press Magazine,* both of which were later resold to the *Fort Wayne News–Sentinel* and then to *Right Here* travel magazine.

I've written about the Grand Ole Opry for *Stereo,* about the Country Music Hall of Fame for *International Musician,* and about the Country Music Disc Jockey Convention for *Guitar Player,* and all of these articles were based on one trip to Nashville, Tennessee. You can have the same sort of writing success based on your travels if you plan ahead well.

In order to make your trips pay for themselves, you must go prepared. You need to take your camera, color and black-and-white film, a battery-operated cassette tape recorder, several blank tapes, maps, travel guides, and lists of questions to ask local residents wherever you stop.

Before embarking, study the travel magazines. Buy copies at your local newsstand. Examine their writing styles, and query some of their editors on ideas you have for unique travel features. Send for their writer's guidelines so that you can know their pay rates and the topics they specialize in.

Most travel articles provide basic information: where to stay, which restaurants are the finest or most reasonable, how to anticipate weather, where to find recreational facilities, and what travel restrictions may be in force. Some of the articles may include a brief history of the areas, including two or three amusing anecdotes.

Maintain a travel journal. Throughout each day, make as many journal entries as possible. The more you have to draw upon, the more you will be able to write. Here are some key things to note in your journal:

- local expressions, clichés
- area businesses
- impressions, feelings
- flowers, landscape
- local foods, delicacies
- lakes, rivers, streams
- forests, parks, wildlife
- tourist traps
- fairs, contests, sports
- amusement parks, beaches
- farms, gardens
- landmarks
- cabs, buses, trains
- prices, fees, tips

To get a feel for a place, read the local newspapers and clip items of odd, humorous, or special news. Stop by the local chamber of commerce or auto club and pick up booklets, flyers, brochures, and maps related to the area. If a state park or federal wildlife area is nearby, obtain copies of the government pamphlets printed about these areas.

Make sensory notes about the towns you go through. What did the Swedish bakery smell like in Minneapolis? What did the hills look like in Pittsburgh?

What did the music sound like in New Orleans? What did the cotton candy feel like at the fair in Indianapolis? How did the tacos taste in Santa Fe?

Use your tape recorder to catch the spiel of a tour guide, to interview a life-long resident of the area, or to catch the remarks of other tourists. Ask these people what goes on in the area, and ask them to be specific about times, prices, and locations. Street vendors, shop owners, and café owners are also good people to interview, especially if you can pick up a new recipe.

With your camera you can catch genuine sights. Look for words spelled in flowers, signs on barns, antique weather vanes, funny graffiti and bumper stickers, curious signs in shop windows, activity at flea markets, and other eye-catching scenes that provide great local color, even when shot in black and white. If, however, you need professional photos of overseas locations, glossy prints can be obtained from consulates and tourist bureaus.

One seasoned traveler I know begins to put her travel articles together even while on the trip. She writes detailed letters to her friends and relatives about her adventures and then keeps a copy of each letter for herself. These later form the basis of her travel features once she gets home.

Another travel writer takes six large envelopes with her when she leaves on vacation and addresses each envelope to herself. When she stops at a resort town or tourist area, she puts her cassette-taped interviews, journal notes, brochures, and flyers into one envelope and mails it back to herself. Then she drives on to the next stop. Two weeks later when she arrives home, six packets are waiting to be opened. Her travel notes are already separated and can be tackled one feature at a time.

Truly, the organized traveler/writer can have fun while also earning bylines and royalties. So, the next time you have to go out-of-state to visit your relatives, just smile. Even *that* trip can be profitable.

IDEAS FOR FICTION

By now you may be thinking, *This is all great for nonfiction writing, but I also want ways to come up with fiction topics.* Well, say no more. If you ever run out of fiction ideas, just pick up your daily newspaper and you will find twenty or thirty plot ideas.

Advice Columns

Read the letters to "Ann Landers" and "Dear Abby" and try to retell the problems presented as short stories. Ignore the response letters, and imagine how your story version would resolve itself from your perspective. Many recent bestsellers have plots similar to problems discussed in advice columns.

Check the business advice columns, too. You should be able to get a plot idea from a letter that begins, "Now that Dad's pension fund has been exposed as being bust and our final mortgage payment is due…"

Comic Strip Shuffle

Take five dramatic comic strips and cut out all the squares in the various panels and shuffle them. Flip them up at random, lay them end-to-end, and read the story. You will wind up with something like Rex Morgan, M.D., appealing to Daddy Warbucks for funds to keep Mary Worth's retirement condominium from being closed, which is really not a bad plot. Concerned physician helps change his father's ruthless corporate image by convincing him to help keep senior citizens from being evicted from their apartments. One of the grateful women apartment dwellers goes to meet the capitalist in order to express her gratitude. They fall in love and marry, and Daddy and Mary live happily ever after.

Comic Strip Rewrites

Cover up the word bubbles in the comic strips and try to put your own story to the visual scenes. Ask yourself, "Why would a strong Rex Morgan be tackling a helpless child?" Is a speeding truck about to hit the child? Is Rex a bully? A kidnapper? All of the above?

Book Reviews

Turn to the arts page and read a review of a book you have not read. Most reviewers will not spoil a book for you by revealing its ending. So, take the skeleton of the review and use it to outline the beginning of a story that you will develop your own way. Your original ending, different locale, and characters will ensure the uniqueness of the story, particularly if it's a story of one genre (Western? Gothic?) that you intend to write in a different genre (romance? mystery?).

Letters to the Editor

A public forum or letters to the editor column produces a variety of ideas for plots. Here's one: "To the Crazed Maniac Who Ran Down Our Three-Year-Old Daughter Last Tuesday on Elm Street and Didn't Stop: I'm after you and if it takes me a lifetime I'll find you. Give yourself up now to the police or prepare to face me soon." Or how about this: "Can't the old public library be saved? I know it's small, but that makes it quaint. I know it's ancient, but that makes it a landmark. I know it's drafty, but that makes it a good place to hold hands with your special gal. I know. I've been doing that for fifty-one years now with my Bessie. It would just kill us to see the old place knocked down and replaced by a parking lot for the local mall."

The first letter is a great plot for a revenge story you could call "Vendetta for Little Amy." The second letter could be expanded into a story after a little brainstorming. The writer of the letter could be a retired handyman. To protect the library from destruction, he could plead with the wrecking crew, hide the fuses to the dynamite, and mail letters to the demolition crew members protesting the job. Eventually, he might get the entire town to rally behind him.

These five tips will get you started. With careful exploring, you may be able to find other plot ideas hidden at various places in your daily newspaper. So be careful not to line the birdcage with your next bestseller.

AUTOBIOGRAPHY

Do not overlook your own life as a potential source of ideas, illustrations, feature articles, short story plots, and even books. What sorts of things do you like to read about? What issues interest you? What difficulties have you confronted in your life that might be of value to others? Have you faced illness? Child rearing difficulties? Have you found a solution to a tricky housecleaning problem? If there's something you have faced, then chances are that others have faced the same problem. So, write from your life experience.

A few autobiographies make it as books on their own. It is not impossible. If you have a unique story, or an unusual perspective, or if you are well known, then your autobiography has potential as a book—ask James Evans, a man with dyslexia and attention deficit hyperactivity disorder who at age twenty-two wrote his autobiography, *Uncommon Gifts,* which tells about growing up learning disabled. But even if you do not have a marketable autobiography, your life story can still provide writing material. Here are some suggestions for writing up and organizing your autobiographical stories.

Prior to writing up your autobiographical material, read several varied examples of this genre. I suggest *The Diary of Anne Frank, The Autobiography of Benjamin Franklin, Iococca* by Lee Iococca and William Novak, and *Angela's Ashes* by Frank McCourt. All four of these books are autobiographies, yet each is vastly different in style and format. They show you the amazing range of approaches open to this form of writing.

To begin writing, separate your life into natural time segments. You can use infancy, childhood, adolescence, and early/middle/late adulthood. Perhaps, instead, you would like to divide your life into five-year segments. Another approach might be to separate your life according to places you have lived. Use whatever sequence is most applicable to your life.

Next, list the time-period headings on pieces of notepaper, such as "1995–2000" or "The Business Years" or "Middle Adulthood: Ages 35–60." Under each heading, list every random memory, personal experience, important person's name, and major event pertaining to that period. Afterward, you can make new versions of these lists and put the random ideas in chronological order.

With your life divided into periods, you can begin to flesh out each era. You may wish to relax in an easy chair, look at your reminder list, and talk into a tape recorder about each phase of your life. You can later transcribe your tapes. If you prefer to write in longhand or to use a computer, that's fine, too.

As you write about each era, you will need to assess the value of the various items on each list. Some items will merit long, detailed explanations, whereas others will only be worth a hasty mention.

As the weeks pass, you will accumulate many pages of copy. This, however, will not produce a unified story. For that you will need to start with the first segment and rewrite it. In the rewriting, insert some foreshadowing elements (teasers) about what will be told later in the narrative. Also, add some long-running elements that can be carried through from one era to the next as a unifying factor, such as your never-ending battle to lose weight or your unshakable belief that one day you would find your long-lost father. Work hard at making the ending of one phase of your life flow nicely into the beginning of the next phase.

In brainstorming about what to include in your autobiography, surround yourself with prompters: high-school yearbooks, family photo albums, scrapbooks, trophies, military uniforms, cheerleader outfits, plaques, 4-H ribbons, letters, and mementos from your travels.

Call several of your friends and relatives and ask them to help you recall aspects of your first family reunion or the night you were elected a class officer or the day you scored the winning touchdown. Write out your personal philosophy of life and include it, too.

Once it is completed, share your autobiography or portions of it with someone special. Ask for a reaction. If certain parts prove to be especially entertaining for another reader, consider developing them into vignettes or short stories or feature articles for freelance sales.

Your autobiography also allows you to pass down to succeeding generations a record of your life and the times in which you lived. You will be able to record feelings of gratitude to God, country, neighbors, and family members for blessings you have received; thus, your autobiographical material can be a tribute.

Keep in mind that every age is the right age for autobiographical writing. When W. Somerset Maugham was sixty-five, he wrote his life story. It was called *The Summing Up*. It sold very well. Its only flaw was that it was too eager to be all-inclusive. It didn't sum up at all. You see, after the book was released, Maugham went on to live to be ninety-one.

CHAPTER FOUR

Expanding Your Writing Vistas

Although the creative aspects of writing cannot be systematized, many of the methods by which topics can be "discovered" can be reduced to systematic procedures, as we saw in chapter three. Now, we will examine ways in which we can use those procedures to project topics on a more long-range basis. After all, what you write today will need to be newsworthy when it is published one to six months from now (or two years in the case of books).

A writer draws on the *past* in order to write *currently* about the *future* concerns of readers. This juggling act of interchanging time realms can be confusing if an author does not have a grasp of the procedures for gauging trends and foreseeing where they will lead in the future. In this chapter we will look at the writers' methods for staying on the cutting edge of news developments. Let's begin by discovering how writers can learn to be futurists and then adapt this talent to developing writing projects.

THE FUTURIST WRITER

No one, not even writers, can predict the future. Nevertheless, many writers do know how to gauge social and cultural developments and, thereby, accurately anticipate pending news evolvements. In writing my book *Millennium Approaches* (Avon, 1998) I reported on developments and trends in such areas as technology, education, sports, the arts, politics, and family life. Writers who do this sort of anticipatory reporting are called futurists. Their talents for foreseeing trends and developments help them to know exactly what topics they should be writing about. It's not a simple challenge, however. There are difficulties. Let me explain.

The future comes upon us *so* quickly that certain predictions seem to be ancient history by the time they are published. Consider this example: As visionary and all-inclusive as Alvin Toffler's book *Future Shock* appeared to be in 1970, it did not even anticipate or predict the two most stunning, newsworthy developments of contemporary society—genetic engineering and microprocessing. Journalists like Toffler have always been thought of as the lookouts and point men for historians. Of late, however, some of the point men and women have become historians of sorts.

In the three to six months it takes to research, write, and get a magazine article into print, numerous new breakthroughs take place in many fields. Many "current" magazine features are outdated before they hit the stands. Books fare even worse. This puts a greater and greater responsibility on freelance writers to catch trends early, obtain the most up-to-date facts possible, and assimilate projections and opinions from trustworthy sources.

It is almost impossible to grasp how fast things are actually changing today. Even *speed* itself is a newsworthy topic. Charles Lindbergh flew solo across the Atlantic Ocean in thirty-three-and-one-half hours in 1927; today, the space shuttle can do the same thing in nine minutes. In 1909 an automobile reached 25 miles per hour; in 1959 the X-15 rocket plane reached 2,500 miles per hour; in 1969 the Apollo spacecraft reached 25,000 miles per hour.

According to author and futurist Tom Sine, "We writers are in a Charles Dickens scenario. We live in the best of times, the worst of times. Unfortunately, we often can't tell which is which. To serve our readers, we are going to have to study more divergently, question more intently and observe more keenly. Only then will our writings remain timely."

Harold Pluimer, author of *The Frontiers of Our Time,* told me, "As writers, we either evolve or dissolve. To evolve, we must master not only the new technology of our field, such as word-processing, but also the new reporting. This new reporting requires that writers discover *now* what the news of the future will be and then report on it as (or before) it happens."

FACING CONTINUOUS CHANGE

The job of modern writers is to meet the emotional and/or educational needs of readers. To do this, writers must be attuned to the ever-evolving social environment. Things have never stayed the same; however, since 1957—the year of Sputnik—things have been changing in major ways on a weekly basis. The last five decades have seen developments never before experienced by mankind.

Socially

The nuclear family (dad, mom, brother, sister) has been replaced by sixty-two different family forms, ranging from unmarried professional women who want children but not husbands to extended families composed of two divorced parents now remarried and starting a new family of "yours, mine, and ours." Readers are seeking articles and books on how to cope with such erratic and new situations.

Financially

America's middle class has begun to disappear now that layoffs and high taxes have made discretionary income almost a thing of the past. Today, people are either very well off or they are constantly struggling to make ends meet. The financially comfortable family of the 1950s has long ago disappeared. How these financial extremes will affect society and its families are topics authors will need to address.

Politically

We have developed an international Us versus Them mentality regarding everyone from the people of the former Soviet Union and Cuba to Libya and Iraq. No one seems to trust anyone anymore. Naturally, the traditional American approach to global politics has been to offer peace and optimism, but that will now need to be redefined and examined by competent writers.

Biologically

Experiments with DNA have made cloning possible in farm animals. The next phase will be to duplicate this success with other animals. If tried with humans, the threat and promise of a master race will need to be dealt with once again. Writers will need to confront these situations from both an ethical and a scientific perspective.

Psychologically

The micro-video-robotics boom has made the concept of Big Brother a current reality and a constant threat. Privacy has been abolished. People now know there is no place to hide in which a heat sensor, laser camera, ultra-sensitive microphone, or directional sonar device cannot locate them. Military satellites can photograph a bicyclist in Chattanooga at midnight. How this will affect the privacy of the home and community will make for a multitude of writing opportunities.

Economically

The population of the world is so poverty stricken that on any given day there are seventy million people suffering from malnutrition and on the verge of starving to death. Those in many African nations also have dangerously short supplies of water, and AIDS is killing the population there at a rate that is rising exponentially each year.

Religiously

Churches are dividing into three factions. The three factions that I see are the adventists, who say the kingdom of God is at hand, the incarnationists, who say the kingdom of God is within us, and the opportunists, who say the fields are white for harvest in regard to winning converts. To discern the differences and explain the factions, writers will need to be talented and diligent.

NEWS WRITING GOALS

Bob Dylan was a futurist in 1963 when he sang, "The times, they are a changin'." Anymore, change is the only thing that remains constant. This applies to writing, too. Tom Wolfe's "new journalism" *(The Right Stuff)* and Truman Capote's "nonfiction novel" *(In Cold Blood)* have proved that writing styles can and will adapt to the times. Even new formats, such as books on disk and books on audio tape, show that change is everywhere. To earn a living as a writer, one must stay current and aware of changes.

Writing during this new century is expected to contain more heart than ever before. Instead of just the five *W*s (who, what, when, where, why), writing will also need to include a *Q* for quality, a *D* for diversity, an *R* for rationality, an *E* for evaluation, and an *S* for style.

Editor and author Philip Yancey *(What's So Amazing About Grace?)* has noted, "We have been easy on ourselves for too long. It's time we writers realized that the quality of our work becomes an integral part of its message." Yancey believes that the good writing of the future will not only present ideas and thoughts, but also "the personalities involved and the context of how those thoughts developed." In short, writing will move toward presenting material with both depth and charm.

Harold Pluimer has observed, "We need a new richness in our written expression. We are a very linguistically splintered society. Right now 104 different languages are being spoken in the city of Los Angeles. If we writers can become more diverse in our realm of knowledge, while also focusing deeply on areas of major concern, our articles and books will remain useful and powerful even when translated."

John R. Ingrisano, president of Poetica Press Publishing Company, claims that small publishers like himself have begun to seek a moral tone and a rational style in newly submitted manuscripts. He says, "Tomorrow's readers are going to want more than just facts. They are also going to want value judgments, structured assessments, and mature counsel. It will not be enough, for example, to report on the legal aspects of a living will; readers will also want to know how religious, social, and moral standards will be affected by such a document. There's a fine line between an author's personal opinion and his or her reports on the norms of society. It will take skillful writers to walk that line. Companies like mine are already looking for such writers."

There are several ways a writer can become a futurist; the key, however, is in being *alert*. The more alert a writer is to the emotional problems, social concerns, and physical needs of human beings, the more apt he or she will be to anticipate forthcoming changes.

Futurist writers should comb the yellow pages and newspaper want ads to discover new businesses and then become acquainted with the businesses' accompanying technology. These writers should travel to different areas to gain regional and cultural perspectives on social developments. They also should review the past by screening newsreels or perusing old magazines to discover universal trends.

Most importantly, writers should look at their own lives and ask, "What are my own concerns about the future?" This will provide an area to explore and to write about, as well as an incentive for following through on the project.

The *Gone with the Wind* character Scarlett O'Hara repeatedly said, "I'll worry about that tomorrow." For the freelance writer, tomorrow often comes *today.* We need to be ready for it. But let's look now at how we can anticipate the news trends of tomorrow before they arrive today.

CATCHING TRENDS

I have found that in freelance magazine writing, catching trends is like bulldogging calves—either you hit them fast or they leave you in the dust. Freelancers have to watch for developing lifestyle and writing trends with the same eagerness and attentiveness that the cowboy waits for a bull to rush from a rodeo pen. Here is the problem: Magazine issues are planned from 45 to 150 days or more in advance. Books have an even longer planning stage, needing one to two years for preparation and production. In effect, what you are submitting to magazines in the spring has to be "news" when it hits the stands in late summer or early fall. What you are submitting to book publishers has to be timely one year after its acceptance by a publisher. And unless you are a prophet or are well enough known to personally *begin* a trend, you are going to need a system for predicting next season's interests. I have four suggestions for anticipating trends.

Read Newspaper Editorials
Editors not only are very sensitive to changes in society, they also are coherent in their explanations of them and outspoken in their opinions on them. Back in 1978, by checking back through editorials I had clipped and saved for six months, I found four different editors who had discussed the technological bene-

fits Americans had gained from the space program of the 1960s. This indicated a possible rising new interest in further space research programs. I immediately contacted NASA press officials and my area congressional representatives for updates on America's interest in space. I was amazed to find out we still had many projects worth pursuing, including the Mars probe and new trips for the space shuttle. My subsequent article, "Space Pace: On the Drawing Boards, but in a Holding Pattern," was purchased by a small Midwestern newspaper chain and used in nine daily newspapers.

I recommend that you clip editorials from both large and small circulation newspapers. Make sure the papers are divergent in political leanings, too. This way, if you find something being discussed by both rural and urban editors and by both Democratic and Republican sympathizers, you will know you have caught a universal trend. I subscribe to three Indiana newspapers, and I spend one day a week in the library reading out-of-state papers. I make notes of interesting commentaries, and I photocopy any outstanding editorials.

Monitor Letters to the Editor

Let's say you read the following letter in your local paper:

> I'm beefed about the way our Great American Pastime is being ignored by today's kids. I love baseball. I grew up playing sandlot ball and collecting Cal Ripkin bubble gum cards. It was great fun. Nowadays, these youngsters are putting on hippie headbands and silky hotpants and playing soccer. That's not American! I say we go back to developing more guys like Ken Griffie, Jr., and Mark McGwire.

At first glance you might smile and dismiss this as the writing of some guy who needed to blow off a little steam. A closer look, however, might make you wonder if some of what he says may be true. He might be right about the rise in popularity of soccer. And if that's a trend, you need to check on it.

You could phone some Little League coaches to ask if participation is down; you could contact summer playground directors to ask which is being used more, baseballs or soccer balls; and you could question youngsters in your own neighborhood about their sports preferences. You might discover that a real trend is developing in favor of soccer.

Remember that people who are set in their ways are usually the first to complain about things that alter their established lifestyles. So, by reading letters to the editor or by listening to radio call-in shows and televised editorial rebuttals from citizens, you have good opportunities to become aware of trends and changes.

Focus on Specialized News Periodicals

Though it's less obvious, these are an important source of trend indicators. Most of us subscribe to a daily newspaper and listen to TV and radio news reports. These media outlets, however, only feature generalized news; that is, they focus on items that affect the majority of people on that particular day. That's good for now, but it does you little good in predicting the news of tomorrow or next year. For that, you need to expand your reading scope.

I make it a practice to skim the tables of contents of several dozen small circulation specialty publications whenever I'm in the library. Just before the natural foods fad was in full swing, I saw an article in a farming journal on how to roast acorns and an article in a camping publication on six ways to make dandelion leaves edible. That gave me an idea. I did some more research and eventually sold an article called "Don't Mow Your Yard—Eat It!" to a national publication. I jumped in early on what soon became a very big dietary trend for many people.

What do you look for in the specialized periodicals? Look for *pending trends.* Here are some to consider:

Focus on plant life. Plants give us oxygen, food, drugs, chemicals, fertilizer, and burnable fuel, all of which our overcrowded planet will need in ever-increasing quantities during the next decades. Articles about scientific research on plants will be popular if written in lay language. Stress benefits.

Focus on increasing tax headaches. Few people will be earning more in spendable money (what economists term *real dollars*), but inflation may kick us into higher tax brackets. Any article on tax write-off benefits will be marketable copy.

Focus on disease breakthroughs. Expect continuous announcements of new immunizations or cures for allergies, AIDS, flu strains, and certain forms of cancer. Explanations of these new drug treatments and interviews with physicians and scientists knowledgeable in these areas will make salable copy.

Focus on the new homemaker. Look for some working mothers and career women to begin dropping out of the full-time work force. They will revamp their home life to make it less routine and more rewarding. Some will use home-based computers, e-mail, fax machines, Web sites, and teleconferencing to continue corporate work or consulting careers without having to leave their homes. Articles on these new "family centers" (homes) will be controversial, yet topical and very marketable.

Focus on senior groups. Gray Power will become even more vocal as longevity increases and Social Security lags behind inflation. Lobbies by senior citizens will demand new federal research into heart problems and arthritis afflictions; they will demand stricter regulations for retirement home management and pension fund supervision; they will seek to abolish all mandatory retirement ages. Articles on any of these topics will be marketable.

Get Clues from People Who Are Involved in Creative Projects

When I was younger, I somehow got the crazy notion in my head that dress designers didn't want to discuss their ideas for next year's clothes and authors didn't want to discuss a work-in-progress and scientists didn't want to talk about their experiments until they were proved right. But that isn't necessarily true.

Usually, it is the reverse that is true. For example, I called a geologist recently and said, "I understand that you are an authority on land revitalization. One of your colleagues told me you were spending this summer in the Arizona badlands. Are you planning on conducting any experiments there?" The geologist talked to me for an hour on the phone and, later, three more hours during an office appointment about a decrystalization-of-sand theory he had. There was no turning him off. He truly enjoyed his role as the knowledgeable authority.

I make many such phone calls each month. There are six colleges in the city where I live, so, I keep in touch with several professors. I also phone or correspond via e-mail with several politicians, ministers, architects, union directors, and civic leaders. The reason many of the projects and plans these people later announce appear to be so shocking or unexpected is simply because no one ever asked them anything ahead of time. It's up to you as an active freelance writer to contact them, and not the other way around.

In fact, that's your basic rule of thumb in the whole trend-catching process: *Since people set and/or follow trends, you must keep tabs on people.* Find out what newspaper editors are telling people and what the people's responses are to the editors. Find out what the specialty and creative people are writing about or developing. Get your facts written up and submitted before others get word of what is developing. You see, unlike your friends and acquaintances who are offended by the remark, editors just love it when you as a writer can say, "I told you so."

LONG-RANGE TRENDS

Often student writers will ask me to speculate about what the hot new topics will be as we progress further into the twenty-first century. Here are some key areas I feel will be worth tracking:

The Law

In the future, computers will be liable for litigation if they malfunction and do "injury" to a person. Theoretically speaking, a computer could be represented by another computer as legal counsel. What's next? Will computers eventually compose our laws? How will citizens respond to such dehumanizing developments?

Unions

In 1983 the Chrysler Corporation cut its unionized work force nearly in half and then recorded its greatest profits ever in the first quarter of 1984. When General Motors suffered a strike in the summer of 1998, the public learned that the company had cut its work force by 47 percent during the previous fifteen years. One of the most successful corporations is IBM, and it has never been unionized. How will facts like these reshape or perhaps eliminate unions in this new century?

Communications

Fiber optics allows the entire text of the *Encyclopaedia Britannica* to be transferred from Boston to Houston in four seconds and to have it stored on a disk smaller than the palm of one's hand. Will this eventually make traditional libraries obsolete?

Techno-Genetics

Some robots now being used in science and industry are composed of a combination of protein molecules in a saline solution and stainless steel and computer parts. When they need maintenance, they are serviced by both a biologist and a mechanic. Will future, more sophisticated versions of these robots be considered to be "alive" or just machines?

Education

Of five thousand United States schools visited by a survey team in the 1990s, all but two had a sports trophy case visible as soon as visitors entered the school. Presently, ten times as many students take driver's education classes as take calculus or physics. What do these educational priorities say about our future ability to compete in an age of advanced technology? What should writers be reporting to the public in this regard?

WRITING COLUMNS

Now that you know how to predict trends and anticipate the news of the future, you may wish to put those skills to steady use by becoming a columnist. I say this because columnists write about current events that show where we are headed in the future. They analyze, evaluate, and respond to life-shaping occurrences. So, to be a columnist, you need to be both a reporter and a futurist. Let me explain how to go about it.

Your first objective will be to come up with a good idea for a column and then to find a newspaper or magazine that will run your column on a regular basis. As we'll see in a moment, this isn't as difficult as it might seem.

Most readers are familiar with well-known columnists, such as William Buckley, Billy Graham, Carl Rowan, Dave Barry, Ann Landers, and Jane Bryant Quinn, who specialize in one particular area (politics, religion, racial issues, comedy, advice, or finances). These columnists have high visibility because their columns are syndicated through a wire service and are published daily in hundreds of newspapers.

What is more important to you, however, is that there are thousands of other columnists who are also being published regularly, though on a smaller readership basis. All newspapers are on the lookout for writers who can come up with an entertaining or informative concept for a column that can be sustained for a long time. So, too, are editors of religious magazines, church publications, and denominational periodicals.

When I first became interested in active freelance writing, I approached the editor of the *Muncie Star* newspaper with the idea of letting me write a column about music. I submitted five sample columns. After reading the columns, the editor agreed to give the column a chance. Under the name "Music News and Views," my columns ran for five Saturdays. Response from the readers was so positive, I was allowed to continue the column for the next two years. Later, I also began a column called "Dust Jacket Reviews" for the Sunday edition in which I profiled authors and reviewed new books.

To get started as a columnist, sit down for a moment and make a list of all the subjects you feel you know a great deal about. This is where you can have real enjoyment from writing because you can select topics to research and write about that are of greatest interest to you. Columns now appearing in local newspapers cover such topics as dog grooming, travel, cooking, gardening, retirement, crafts, hobbies, investments, real estate, medicine, hunting, home decorating, sewing, sports, the arts, politics, and marriage counseling. Columns in religious magazines focus on questions about the Bible, family life, marital harmony, Christian singles, ministries, church management, and pastoral training. No doubt your list will contain an equal or greater variety of subjects.

From your list, focus on the topic you know best and enjoy writing about most. Take five aspects of this topic and prepare one column (approximately 250 to 750 words) on each aspect. Submit these five columns to your local newspaper or specialty magazine along with a cover letter explaining your writing experience and your experience related to the subject of your column.

Allow the newspaper editor a week to respond to you. For a magazine, wait up to four weeks for a response from the editor. If you do not receive a letter or phone call, you then may wish to call or visit the editor to see if there was any interest in your column idea. If not, don't be discouraged. Just submit your sample columns to another newspaper or magazine, and then another, until you find an editor who is interested in your column.

Although a column for a local newspaper or small circulation magazine may not pay as well as you would like (pay ranges from $15 to $80 per column) it will provide several additional benefits. You will get a lot of writing experience and a lot of exposure for your byline; you will become well known as an expert in a certain field and this will open doors for you when you want to write freelance articles for national magazines that specialize in that field; and you will begin to amass a series of informative clippings you later may be able to develop into a book.

If your column is very successful in your local paper, you later can submit samples of it to the various wire services. If your writing style has reader appeal and your column has broad reader interest, you may one day find yourself among the ranks of the nationally syndicated columnists.

In regard to writing style, columnists have no journalistic elbowroom. They cannot meander. So, when in doubt, cut copy. The reader doesn't have to become an authority on your topic. He or she just wants facts. Try to summarize in one sentence what each new column will focus on. What are you trying to prove, solve, expose, or share? What are your sources to support your claims? What group is your target reading audience?

Keep your paragraphs brief. Use strong, vivid verbs and eliminate most adjectives and adverbs, except in situations where one adverb can replace several other words. (Example: "The spy moved quickly" is better than "The movements of the spy were quick.")

Write, rewrite, and cut. Make every word justify its existence. Decide upon the point you want to make and stay on the topic. Your goal will be to convey information in an interesting way. Use short, specific words.

The more specialized a column is, the more difficult it will be to keep it fresh, lively, and nonrepetitive. It's best to establish at least six subtopic areas upon which you can comment in rotation so that no single category gets too much attention.

For two years I wrote a column called "Shopkeeper's Keys" for *Craft and Needlework Age* magazine. The column offered advice on how to manage craft, quilting, and sewing shops. I rotated the column's focus among six subcategories: advertising, publicity, new products, personnel management, cash flow systems, and clientele service. This gave the column uniformity in theme (small-store management) but allowed a great diversity of topics for discussion.

To maintain a wellspring of ideas for columns, you must create a file system. Label folders or disks with a variety of categories, such as education, television, music, politics, money, vacations, food, war, and holidays. Fill these folders with newspaper and magazine articles related to the topics. Also file unique advertisements, filler items, and letters to the editor that relate to the topics. Save any notes you take from a public speech, college lecture, TV or radio show, or reference book.

These ready files will save hours of research time and will provide stimuli for topics to focus on in your columns. Before putting a magazine article or other item into a file, date it, and note its source. Read it carefully, and underline the key passages in red (or another easily distinguishable color) so that you only need to scan it later. If one article could be filed in two different folders, file it in one, and note a cross reference on the outside of the other folder. For example, an article on the salaries of teachers could be filed in the "teachers" file and cross-referenced in the "public education" file. If you keep your files on computer and scan the articles, be sure that you keep backup copies on disks in case something happens to your hard drive.

The serious columnist will make an effort to reveal unknown facts, focus on new trends, and announce recent breakthroughs in relation to the column's main focus. To obtain this information the columnist will need to interview experts in the field, study both major and lesser-known trade journals, and read the specialized books and periodicals being released that relate to the main topic.

During the past ten years I have maintained active columns in a variety of newspapers and magazines. Being a columnist has provided me with a steady monthly income, a sizable amount of personal publicity, a good excuse for spending many hours reading, and ready access to almost anything I wished to attend ("I'm here to cover this for my column"). I recommend it to any writer who is seeking steady writing challenges, regular work, and continuous exposure.

Initially, you may have picked up this book and wondered if it could help you write the one big story on your heart and mind. Now you realize that you not only can write that story, but you also can continue to find dozens of other topics to write about. Look for ideas, and you will discover them.

Never overlook the stories that appear before you every day. Sometimes the most common trials in our daily lives can lead to very profound stories. One of the first short stories I ever sold was to a Sunday-school paper, and it was about an old church janitor who took pride in being "the caretaker of God's own house." That story was based on the life of the custodian of my church, a man whose original plans to be a minister had been redirected after he suffered a crippling accident as a teenager. After that story was published, I was approached by many people who told me it had helped them see that what we want for our lives is not always what God has in mind for us. My belief is that we must seek His will first.

In the next section we are going to engage in an in-depth study of how to write in a professional way. This may be the most challenging and most interesting phase of your development as a freelance writer. Thus far, you have learned how to prepare yourself for a full- or part-time career in writing, and you have learned where to discover things to write about. Now, let's get those keyboards or ink pens in motion. It's time to start the actual writing itself.

PART III

Writing with Style and Impact

I don't know whether you have ever stopped to think about it, but the written pages that have had the most influence on changing people's lives have all been short, deliberate, and powerful. The Lord's Prayer has only 56 words. Abraham Lincoln's Gettysburg Address is only 266 words long. The Ten Commandments combined amount to just 297 words. Even the Declaration of Independence has fewer than 300 words. Amazing, isn't it? To think that so much content could be contained in so few words! And yet, as we shall see in this section, that is one of the keys to success in freelance writing: *making every word count for something.*

Do you select each word carefully? Are you a confident writer? Do you believe you have a message on your heart that you need to share with the reading public? Or are you faint-hearted and fearful that you may not have what it takes to become a word-conscious writer?

As a beginning writer you may think you have nothing going for you. You probably feel that the odds are stacked heavily against you. There is another way of looking at it, however. You could be like the coach who told his team, "You men are unbeaten, untied, and unscored upon. Now let's get out there and play that first game!"

You are in a similar position. Today begins your new season. You are unrejected, unrefused, and undefeated. So, let's get out there and sell that first manuscript!

It's within your grasp. It doesn't matter what your situation is. Many people have proven that. Jack London was a grade-school dropout who later became the first person in history to earn a million dollars solely by freelance writing.

Catherine Marshall was a preacher's widow when she wrote *A Man Called Peter.* Sir Arthur Conan Doyle and W. Somerset Maugham gave up careers as medical doctors in order to write full time. Margaret Mitchell was a newspaperwoman before she wrote *Gone with the Wind.* John Bunyan was a prisoner when he wrote *Pilgrim's Progress.*

The only common denominator among all successful writers is the ability to communicate effectively. That, after all, is what good writing really is—the ability to get an idea out of your head and onto a piece of paper in so clear a manner that it will go into the reader's head and provide enlightenment or entertainment. *Communication* is a writer's one-word credo.

Though many of us *think* we are communicating effectively, the fact is that we often are not. I am reminded of the story of the three elderly men who were sure they didn't need hearing aids. They were riding a train from London to Wembley. When they arrived at the station, one old man asked, "Is this Wembley?" The guy next to him said, "No, you old goat, it's Thursday!" The third man looked up and said, "I am, too! Let's get off here and get a lemonade."

Like these three men, too many would-be writers are unable to communicate effectively. It's not enough to *assume* your ideas are being understood, you must *know* that they are understood.

How do we begin to communicate effectively? Most writing classes start by having students pick up their pens and begin to write an essay or a short story. That can be an overwhelming request. It's like handing someone a hammer and asking him or her to build a house. A class in writing, instead, should begin with the simplest, most elemental aspects of writing and then progress to more complicated procedures, with communication and audience being important throughout.

Not only do I feel that starting with the essay or short story is too weighty for writing classes, I even feel that starting with the paragraph or sentence is too much to focus on. The study of writing should begin with an analysis of *words.* So, that's where we will begin: word power. From there, like the house builder, we will learn how to draft a literary blueprint known as an article outline. Once the outline is prepared, we then will learn how to piece together the actual structure (of the article or book) element by element: its title, its lead, its transition, its body, and its closing.

CHAPTER FIVE

Mastering Procedures for Article Writing

Although chapters five and six will focus primarily on nonfiction writing skills and chapter seven will focus primarily on fiction writing skills, many of the basic writing concepts found in all three of these chapters will apply to *both* fiction and nonfiction. This is particularly true of our first topic: learning to use words effectively.

WORD POWER

Consider this: If you hold a dictionary in your hand, you are holding every novel, short story, essay, nonfiction book, and poem ever written. To discover these works, all you have to do is rearrange all the words of the dictionary into the needed patterns.

A writer may be called a "wordsmith," but unlike the blacksmith who makes horseshoes, the writer does not *make* words. Words are already there for writers to use; all the writer needs to do is arrange them on a piece of paper. The key mistake most novice writers make is that they not only arrange words incorrectly but they also select the wrong ones. (One is reminded here of Mark Twain's classic line, "The difference between the right word and the almost right word is the difference between lightning and the lightning bug.")

To ensure that you, the would-be successful freelance writer, will not mis-arrange words or select words incorrectly, you need to *understand* words. It's not enough simply to know the definition of a word, you must also have an understanding of how language history, people's attitudes, and contemporary speaking habits affect the performance of words in a sentence.

Let's consider language history, for example. Today, our common social speech is often casual rather than formal. You don't find people using the language of the King James Version of the Bible in everyday speech. The formal writing of the King James Bible reflected both attitudes and speech patterns of a certain time. And though many Christians have attuned their ears to the rhetoric of the King James Version and understand its language and its rich history of language, they do not use the formality of those words and language patterns to communicate in common, everyday social situations.

To develop word power for today's readers, writers must diligently immerse themselves in current forms of printed communication, such as contemporary magazines, daily newspapers, current novels, and weekly newsletters. Because language is in a constant state of development and expansion, writers must pay careful attention to both the ancient and more recent historical contexts of words.

The writer must also be aware of readers' attitudes toward words and word phrases. Sentences may be grammatically correct and syntactically balanced yet still not communicate effectively. The sentence simply may not "hit the ear" right. For example, a common sentence might be, "Mary hopes to meet an eligible bachelor." Although quaint, that sentence would not raise any eyebrows. However, no one would make the similar statement, "John hopes to meet an eligible spinster." *Spinster* is an offensive term that is used only as an insult these days.

Or take this example. To make a question of any sentence that employs the either/or combination, a singular pronoun must be used. We write, "Either Tim or Bob will stay, won't *he?*" Changing gender from masculine to feminine causes no difficulty since we can write, "Either Linda or Diane will stay, won't *she?*" However, we run into difficulty in our language when we mix genders. To be grammatically correct, we could write, "Either Tim or Linda will stay, won't *he?*" However, that sentence obviously engenders an absurdity. Despite grammatical acceptability, it fails to communicate what we really want to say.

To avoid using those sorts of awkward sentences, most successful writers habitually read their writings aloud. In this way they not only *see* how the words look on the page, they hear the way the words hit the ear. In this process from time to time they discover something that sounds odd or incorrect and make the appropriate changes.

A good writer listens carefully to what people say because correct utilization of habits is important to the writer's finished product. The writer learns that certain audiences require adjectives such as *divine, sweet, adorable, lovely,* and *charming,* whereas other audiences use adjectives such as *great, dynamic, out-standing,* or *terrific.* Different audiences require different types of writing: male or female, teen or senior citizen, highly educated or less so, urban or rural or "burb." People do not express themselves uniformly, and that is important for a writer to remember.

Consider this: A pinkish shade of purple may be called "mauve" by some women or men who are interior decorators, but if you're writing about a steel worker or a truck driver, he is unlikely to say, "Don't you just love our mauve drapes?" He is more likely to say, "Not bad purple curtains, are they?" The writer who ignores these distinctive speaking preferences is doomed to turn out stilted or artificial prose.

WORD POWER IN ACTION

Once you are convinced you need to respect words as the key elements in your freelance writing career, you then will be ready to put words to use. As I stressed earlier, your function as a writer is to communicate. You are not out to try to impress an editor with your six-syllable vocabulary words nor are you out to "snow" readers with obscure terms, legalese, churchology, mumbo jumbo, or academese. You simply want to be able to write in so straightforward a manner that you cannot be misunderstood.

The easiest way to communicate effectively is to write simply and directly. Somerset Maugham noted in *The Summing Up,* "I am proud to say, no one has ever had to run to a dictionary while reading one of my stories." Far too often, novice writers are as conspicuous in their use of long or obscure words as second graders are in the habit of putting exclamation points at the end of each sentence. Good writers say things in as common and as comfortable a way as possible; they visit with the reader.

Consider the way most people talk. In general conversations, sentences are rather short, vocabulary is basic, and topics are focused and limited. Speaking and writing are not identical media, but they are so closely related it becomes impossible for the former not to influence the latter. So, to become better writers, we should see what positive things we can borrow from conversation patterns. Let's begin by looking at simplified vocabulary.

Although studies do not agree on an exact figure, linguists tell us that most people use a basic daily vocabulary of approximately 500 words. If we consider the fact that *Webster's New Collegiate Dictionary* contains more than 416,000 words, we see how few words we use of the great pool available to us. Nevertheless, it's reality; and since writers both analyze and reflect reality, we must recognize that simplified vocabulary is a key element in effective communication with a mass audience.

Use easily understood words. They work in a writer's favor. Why write *avuncular* when *uncle* is much easier to understand? Why write *appurtenances* when more common words, such as *utensils* or *accessories,* are easier for the reader to comprehend?

Use short words whenever possible. This goes along with the idea of simple words being effective. Mark Twain had the idea. He said, "I get paid five cents a word; so, I never give them *metropolis* when *city* will earn just as much." More pertinent, however, is the fact that the reader's eye can dash across a simple two-syllable word like *city,* whereas it must slow down and plod through a four-syllable word like *metropolis* (or worse, a five-syllable word like *megalopolis*). Anytime you can keep the reader's eye zipping through your copy while understanding your content, you are succeeding as a writer.

Use visual nouns. A generic noun such as *house* can become more mentally visual for the reader if it is replaced by *mansion* or *shack.* Similarly, you should use verbs that define the precise action you are trying to explain. Instead of using an ambiguous verb such as *hit,* replace it with something more specific, such as *slapped* or *tapped.*

Vary the sentence patterns and lengths. Instead of writing each sentence in the pattern of subject/verb/object ("Tom went home"), make use of a variety of patterns. You might try a verb/object pattern ("Go home") or an adjective/ subject/verb pattern ("Warm winds blow"). Similarly, although the average journalistic sentence is fifteen words long, your sentences should never be consistent in length. That's hypnotic. Break it up a bit.

Link pronouns clearly to their antecedents. If you use the words *that* or *he* or *it,* make sure the reader clearly knows to what or whom those pronouns refer. Otherwise it gets confusing.

Don't use nouns as adjectives or verbs. Avoid constructions such as "He was a real *car* man" or "We'll *leg* it to work tomorrow." Later, however, we will note that there are exceptions to this rule in creating regional dialogue.

Use active voice whenever possible. The active voice ("Tom gave Bob the book") makes your sentences shorter, and it brings your reader closer to the action than does passive voice ("The book was given to Bob by Tom").

In all that you write, be tough on yourself. Eliminate slow copy; cross out redundancies; double-check grammar and spelling; check the word arrangement in your sentences so that it sounds natural. Test your material by reading it aloud. Make everything you write be the best it can possibly be.

Once you've mastered good writing technique, you can move to the specifics of how to plan, outline, and write an article. The article outline at the end of this chapter will provide a framework on which you can build your articles or evaluate articles you have already drafted. Let's look at the key elements of an article and see how you can make each element work.

Let's begin at the beginning by learning how to select and develop titles.

DEVELOPING A TITLE

Some writers like to put a "working title" on a manuscript just to have it labeled and categorized in their minds. They will go back to the title and revise it after the entire work of writing is done. Other writers like to settle on a perfect title first and use it as a point of reference by which to guide the writing that follows. Either way, coming up with a good title is an important part of the process of professional writing.

Since the title of a book, article, poem, or short story is the first thing a reader sees, it should be a grabber. A good title is both brief and clear. It is catchy and to the point, such as *Dress for Success* or *The Divorce Myth* or *Celebration of Discipline*. Often, the more condensed and powerful a title is, the more impact it will have on readers. For example, consider how much stronger the title *Future Shock* is than the title *The Future of Our World*.

Sometimes an effective title can be reduced to just one word, such as Catherine Marshall's *Christy,* James A. Dickey's *Deliverance,* Michael Crichton's *Airframe,* Peter Benchley's *Jaws,* Frank McCourt's *'Tis,* or Robert Louis Stevenson's *Kidnapped.* The right word combined with the right jacket design can be an incredible sales combination.

A title is a quick commercial for your manuscript. Yours must be clear enough to entice an editor and/or a reader to "buy" the whole work, whether it is an article, a chapter title, or a book.

A bad title cannot kill a great book, but it can slow it down. Flat, bland, lifeless titles can harm even a great book, and they will absolutely kill a moderately well-written book. For example, before it was a TV mini-series, *The Thorn Birds* became an international bestseller as a book only after four years of steady sales and a lot of word-of-mouth recommendations. Surveys showed that the title was a major drawback. It didn't tell readers *anything* about the book because virtually no one had ever heard of the Australian legend of the mythical thorn bird.

Titles should be memorable, and they should be appropriate to the topic. One author titled his book about flying balloons *Up in the Clouds.* It was released in 1969, and bookstore owners refused to order it because they thought the book was about LSD or other mind-altering drugs. In 1973, the publisher changed the book's title to *Hot Air Ballooning Made Easy,* and sales were "lofty."

I suggest that you ask yourself the following seven questions whenever you develop a title for your book or periodical manuscripts:

1. **Can it be pronounced easily?** If you ever write the biography of President Carter's National Security Advisor, Zbigniew Brzezinski, try to keep his name out of the title. Call it *Jimmy and Ziggy* instead. People don't like difficult titles.
2. **Is it interesting?** Titles need pizzazz. You can't expect to have a bestseller titled *Life in Smithville.* Research revealed that until it was

"banned in Boston" and thus received national publicity, Grace Metalious's *Peyton Place* was a bookstore bomb. The reason it had a slow start was primarily due to its bland title.

3. **Does it fit the subject matter?** When in doubt, be obvious. If you write a book about weather control and title it *Cookin' Up a Storm,* you can be sure readers will think it's a standard cookbook. It's better to be point blank, even if it adds words to your title. After all, there have been bestsellers with long titles, such as *How to Succeed in Business Without Really Trying* and *Everything You Always Wanted to Know About Sex but Were Afraid to Ask.*

4. **Is it a corny cliché?** Try to be unique, not repetitive and dull. I have a friend who is an editor at a publishing house that specializes in romance novels. She once told me that each year she receives more than twenty unsolicited manuscripts bearing the identical title *My Love Is Like a Red, Red Rose.* She rejects nearly all of them, and the ones she does buy, she assigns new titles. However, writers will sometimes take a cliché and give it a twist as a way of grabbing the reader's attention, such as the mystery *One Bad Deed Deserves Another.*

5. **Is it too sweet?** Don't try to write a cutie-pie title. Gushy or maudlin titles annoy people. Let's face it, not even a little kid would be interested in a book called *My Life with Duckies and Puppies.*

6. **Does it tell too much?** Readers like some suspense in everything they read. It's what keeps them turning pages. So, don't title your mystery *The Butler Did It* and don't call your romance *They Lived Happily Ever After.*

7. **Is it memorable?** A title that burns itself into the memory of readers will be a title that will continue to draw readers to it. They won't be able to forget it, which, of course, is the objective. In recent years several books have achieved this. James Dobson's *Love Must Be Tough* and Robert Schuller's *Tough Times Never Last, but Tough People Do!* are books with very memorable titles. Jack London's title *The Call of the Wild* is unforgettable.

Having asked yourself these questions and having come to the conclusion that your title is a winner, it is time to test it. Try your title on people. If a person's head turns and his or her eyes light up, you'll know you're on target. However, if a person says politely and calmly, "That's nice," you'll know you need to come up with a new title. So write one. Readers are *entitled* to the best you can offer.

WRITING GRABBER LEADS

Your title may attract attention, but you will need to keep the reader from slipping away from you. To do that, you will have to write an opening paragraph, known as the "lead," that will grab the reader and compel his or her involvement in the story. That is quite a challenge for a beginning writer.

As a writing teacher, I have lectured on campuses everywhere from Florida to Michigan and from Massachusetts to Oregon. I have discovered the one common problem all beginning writers have is not being able to grab the reader's attention quickly.

I always tell students, "Keep in mind that what you write only has about ten seconds to win or lose a reader. If your narrative hook is something fascinating that intrigues the reader, he or she will stay with you. If your opening is unimaginative, slow, or routine, your reader will desert you—and fast!"

Why do I say ten seconds to win or lose? Well, let's use *you* as an example. Let's say you arrive at the dentist's office and are told it will be twenty minutes before you can be seen. You scowl, shrug your shoulders, and flop into a chair. You grab a magazine off the table and begin to thumb through the pages.

You pause at the first article. You glance at its title and read the first two paragraphs of the story but then give up on it. You flip the pages to the next article. The same process occurs.

On the third article, however, you find a captivating title: "Skydiving into the Canals of Venice." The opening paragraph describes a leap from an airplane, a parachute that fails to open, a sense of panic.

You read on and on. Time passes quickly. When the receptionist finally says, "Dr. Adkinson will see you now," you flash her a cutting glance. *How dare she!* You slowly begin to walk toward the inner office, the magazine still in your hand. You've *got* to see how this thing turns out.

That author snagged you and refused to let you escape. She piqued your curiosity, maintained your interest, and pulled you rapidly along the path she wanted you to follow. That's exactly what *you* want to do when you sit down to write a devotional or feature or interview.

Let me show you four surefire methods of how to open your articles with strong reader hooks.

Direct Reader Involvement

One of the most basic, yet continually successful, methods of grabbing the reader's attention quickly is to get the reader directly involved in the article. You do this by avoiding generalities and by pointing a figurative finger into the face of the reader. In short, you address the reader point-blank.

For instance, I once was given the very, very dull assignment of writing a long feature article for a newspaper about how and why a year 2000 census form should be filled out. I realized that the only way I could get anyone to read such an article would be by grabbing the reader's interest with a clever opening statement and then by following it with a series of pointed reasons why *not* filling out a census form could be disadvantageous.

The lead sentence I used was, "It will be the only chance you'll have this entire decade." Right away the reader wondered, "My only chance? What d'ya mean? Chance for what?" To find out, the reader *had* to go on to the next sentence. He was hooked.

Thereafter, the article contained lines such as, "The fewer the number of people reported in an area, the fewer the number of tax dollars there are sent to that area by the federal and state governments. In other words, if you make $35,000 a year, you'll pay about ten cents extra in taxes during the next ten years *for every person* who lives in your area who does not report himself in the census." (Talk money and people listen.)

Anytime you can make the reader feel that the information in your article will have a direct effect on her life, she will stay with you. Get her involved right from the start. Speak directly to the reader. If you answer her question, "What does it have to do with me?" you will hook her early.

The Stunning Statement

Public speakers know the importance of including facts and information in their speeches that keep their listeners whispering, "Wow! I didn't know that.

That's incredible!" The reason such speeches are so captivating is because a writer prepared them that way. As a writer you, too, can use shocking and amazing statements to arrest your reader's attention, while simultaneously relating to him some intriguing information. For example, if you were preparing an article on the problem of government spending, you might use a paragraph such as this:

> A billion seconds ago the Japanese bombed Pearl Harbor. A billion minutes ago Christ was on this earth. A billion hours ago life was first starting to form. A billion dollars ago was yesterday in Washington.

These sorts of facts fascinate the reader, perhaps even scare or dumbfound her. She *must* read on to find out how such a situation developed or how it can be dealt with. You've hooked her. Now all you need to do is supply the answers; she will stay with you until the end.

Name Dropping

If you glance over a magazine stand these days you will see countless periodicals such as *Us, In the Know, Entertainment Weekly,* and *People Weekly.* The number of titles in this genre makes you realize that people love to be told something (anything!) about well-known personalities. Writers who realize this fact can use it to their advantage.

I once wrote a magazine article about how artificial eyes were made and fitted for patients. The eye-making process was interesting, but not anywhere near interesting enough to hook a reader.

So, instead of beginning with technical data about artificial eye manufacturing, I began with a list of names of famous individuals. I wrote, "Actress Sandy Duncan has one, and so does politician Morris Udall. The same goes for Rex Harrison, Peter Falk, and Sammy Davis, Jr. *What* do they have? An artificial eye, that's what!"

That sort of lead fascinates people. Instead of using ambiguous, abstract references, such as "some people have artificial eyes," I used specific, recognizable references when I referred to Sandy Duncan, Morris Udall, and others. Try it. It works.

An Intriguing Anecdote

I sometimes think that early man created the concept of storytelling and then discovered fire just so he could have something to sit around while spinning yarns. We all love stories.

Anecdotes are brief stories that illustrate or amplify a point you are trying to explain. Some anecdotes are parables ("A sower went out to sow"); some are recollections ("My grandfather was an old Indian fighter and my grandmother was an old Indian"); some are jokes ("We put a baptistry at both the front and back of the church so that we could baptize babies at both ends"); and some are sketches or descriptions ("If you want to know about lumberjacks, let me tell you about Paul Bunyan").

Damon Runyon, Ernest Hemingway, Rudyard Kipling, and Jack London often used anecdotes about interesting people as ways to begin their works of journalism or even their short stories. When Hemingway began his short narrative "The End of Something" with the line "In the old days Horton's Bay was a lumbering town," the reader was being presented with a short anecdote to explain why a sparsely populated town now had so many empty buildings. It presented a bit of mystery, intrigue, and irony—and it hooked the reader.

The next time you are facing a blank sheet of paper, not knowing where to begin, try one of these four leads: direct reader involvement, a stunning statement, name dropping, or an intriguing anecdote. Then go sit in a dentist's waiting room and find a patient with a toothache. Test your manuscript lead on him or her.

USING TRANSITIONS

As I said, an outline can serve as a skeleton on which to add the "flesh" of your article, or it can be used generically to evaluate something you have already written. In making the various parts of your outline flow together well, you will need to know how to create smooth transitions. The various parts of the outline don't just automatically blend; they must be helped along.

Have you ever read an article or story that seemed to have its paragraphs stacked atop each other with no connections, like airplanes over La Guardia airport at midday? Boring, isn't it?

Actually, it's worse than boring. It's confusing, tedious, and certainly unprofessional. The problem is a lack of good transitions. The author has not helped you get from one topic to the next. Instead, she has simply spliced together a series of ideas. It doesn't work.

Just as a train can't hold its cars together and run smoothly without couplers, an article or story cannot proceed smoothly without transitions. Transitions help the reader advance from one subject to the next in a natural sequence. They lead the reader to believe that the article or story is proceeding in the only direction it possibly could go.

But trying to create a natural transition is not always easy. We can all recognize stilted transitions, such as those used in old-time movies ("Meanwhile, back at headquarters..."). They stand out like neon signs. They interrupt the flow of an article rather than enhance it. Transitions should be subtle; they should ease readers along in one direction, not kick them along.

Many feature articles, by necessity, call for changes in setting, time, action, and sometimes even subjects. Without smooth transitions, these changes become jolts—and readers hate jolts.

Whether or not you know it, you are already somewhat of a master of transitions. In everyday conversation you constantly use oral transitions like these: "Speaking of funny incidents, that reminds me..." or "If you think *that's* something, you should hear what Shirley did last week..." or "Hey, let me tell you my side of it."

These spoken transitions shift the topic of conversation off in a different direction without completely breaking the original train of thought. They prepare or set up the listener for the story about to be shared. Your written transitions should function in a similar manner. Let's review some of the basic methods of developing transitions.

Comparison and Contrast

The easiest way to move from one subject to the next is to compare or contrast things. For example, if you're moving from a focus on one brother to another brother, you could say, "Since Bob wanted to be just like his brother Bill, he always wore white sneakers, chewed gum, and combed his hair straight back too." This compares the two brothers.

Equally effective would be to contrast the two brothers: "Whereas Bill was fair-haired and tall like his father, Bob had the olive skin and raven hair of his mother." A third option would be to compare *and* contrast the brothers: "Like Bill, young Bobby liked fast cars; but whereas Bill's dreams ended at being a driver, Bobby had ambitions to own the entire speedway."

Turning-Point Questions

A frequently used method of arriving at the answer to a problem raised in an article is the technique of stating the problem as a question. The writer can then proceed to a detailed response.

For example, if you were writing an article about political relations between the United States and Mexico, you might use this transition format:

> Mexico has no nuclear weapons, no standing army of any great merit, no
> submarines, no aircraft carriers, and no major radar installations. Why then
> is the U.S. secretary of state working twenty-four hours a day to secure
> Mexico as a "military" ally?
>> The answer is simple. Oil.
>> Mexico has it and we need it.

A turning-point question focuses the reader's attention on a specific single problem. The only "natural" thing that could follow would be an answer to that problem. Thus, you are able to make the transition from background material to new information without jolting the reader during the shift.

Raised Expectations

One way to move a reader from one paragraph to the next is to suggest that all is not well with your characters or plot. Your reader will then continue to read ahead in expectation of an explanation of the tension. Here's an example of a raised expectation transition:

> As the stranger continued to talk in his casual manner, the sentry made the mis-
> take of assuming the man meant him no harm. He carelessly lowered his rifle.

Although we don't know yet what will happen between the stranger and the sentry, we are prepared for some kind of action to take place. When it does (in the next paragraph), it seems logical to us. The transition prepared us for it.

Correlations

When you need to provide background information or a flashback scene for your reader but don't want to jar the flow of your article or story, you can have your main character see something or pick up something and then correlate that object to the background information. It works this way:

> Tom rubbed the apple against his sleeve. Funny thing about apples. Most
> people associated them with Adam and Eve or William Tell or Isaac
> Newton. But not Tom. Every time he held an apple, he thought of Grandpa
> Ross.

The human senses are constantly sending data to the brain. Since they cause the brain to think of many different things, readers will identify with and accept the use of an object as a stimulant for generating tangent thoughts. By correlating an object to some relevant flashback information, you can ease the reader from the present to the past in your writings.

Summarization

Readers grow weary of repetitious detail in writing. They prefer to have the writing progress rapidly. To accomplish this, you sometimes will have to write transitions that provide brief summaries of background material. Such summaries can quickly get you to the crux of the next action scene. Note this example:

> Mike could feel perspiration forming on his upper lip and forehead. The first
> six innings of the game had been simple. His curve had broken perfectly and
> his fastball had left Deckerville's batters blinking. But now it was different.
> Between innings his shoulder muscle had flared up again.

Here we have summarized the action of the first six innings and, thus, have carefully transported the reader from the beginning of the game to its final innings. The reader has been moved ahead to the real conflict of the article without missing anything of importance along the way. This summarization paragraph leads the reader to assume that the next scene will be a description of Mike's final moments in the game. And, of course, that is exactly what the article will focus on next.

The main thing about transitions is that they must logically direct the reader from one thought to the next in as subtle a manner as possible. Usually, the article itself will help you know which kind of transition to use at a given point. By observing what has been said up to that point in your article, and by knowing the new direction you need to take, you can tell whether a correlation or summarization or some other technique would fit best.

BODY OF THE ARTICLE

The body of the article will contain the key elements of information you wish to convey to your readers. This can be done through the use of statistics, data, research, and references. Such information would not make an article, however, but merely a series of numbers and parts. That is why writers like to quote experts, share anecdotes, present lessons, offer humor, and make suggestions. The body of the article is a stylistic presentation of information in a format that will hold the reader's interest.

ENDING THE ARTICLE

You've progressed from title to lead to transition and through the body of the article. Now you need to know how to end it. When introduced to a stranger, Groucho Marx had a standard reply, "Hello, I must be going." That's what I call getting to the point fast and then closing with finesse.

Too often one of the weakest parts of an article is the ending, or close. Unless the author can conclude with finesse—with the kind of writing that leaves a reader satisfied—the entire manuscript will fall flat. "All's well that ends well" should be a journalistic law.

Most authors focus all their attention on developing a good lead. Their rationale is, "If I can't hook the reader into my story, there's no need to even worry about a close." But that's false logic. For a sustained career, a writer must be as adept at closings as he is at leads. Mystery writer Mickey Spillane once noted that with the balanced book, "The first chapter sells the book; the last chapter sells the *next* book."

In my work as an editor and writing teacher, I have discovered that novice writers think their articles are finished whenever they run out of things to say. Not so. For a piece of writing to be complete, it must provide "take away" value for the reader. That is to say, the reader, upon finishing the article, needs to leave it having gained something in exchange for her time, whether knowledge or entertainment.

Articles must be directed to a *satisfying* close. Endings should have an impact on the reader; they should make the reader feel that she has followed a logical course of events and arrived purposely and correctly at a specific place. It doesn't work for an author just to wave a hand and stutter, "Tha-dit, tha-dit, tha-dit, that's all, folks!" Here are some reasons why closes fail:

- *Situations are unresolved.* Readers are left wondering how things turned out.
- *The close is redundant.* Everything that's already been said is rehashed. (Ho-hum.)
- *The writing becomes listless.* Things just slow to a stop instead of coming to a definite end.
- *The writing becomes prejudiced.* The reader is told what he or she should be thinking. (Just present the facts and keep your opinions to yourself. Don't close with a judgment.)
- *The article and its close are unrelated.* The author goes off on a tangent and makes a concluding remark about the ancillary material.

To avoid these weak closes, I suggest that you keep a "slug sheet" marked *Closes* in your notebook or research file. As you conduct your interviews and dig out your background material for your next article, write down any powerful one-liners, amazing facts, or captivating anecdotes—slugs—that you feel might make good closes for the feature. You can add the slug later to end your article with impact.

When developing a close, I suggest you consider the following techniques, all of which work well when used appropriately:

The Echo Effect

Reread your lead and write a conclusion that answers the problem it presented or one that fully proves the point the lead had made earlier.

The Ironic Twist

Offer a comment that adds a bizarre or unexpected, yet logical, ending to your article. Example: An ex-con who after twenty years of busting rocks on the inside comes out and lands a job at a gravel company.

The Powerful Quotation

A quote from someone featured in your article can often summarize dramatically what your entire article has tried to emphasize. Example:

> "Most preachers give you sermons that tell you 'ya can't take it with ya,'" said the government agent in Guyana, "but the Reverend Jim Jones seems to have had a different idea."

The Joke or Pun

A bit of levity leaves a reader smiling. Appropriate ad libs, puns, jokes, or humorous stories can both summarize a story and provide entertainment.

The Amen Affirmation

A story that presents troublesome yet irrefutable facts can simply affirm the situation and allow the reader to nod understandingly. Example:

> The enemy interrogators had taken away Captain Wilson's freedom, his clothes, his food, and his proximity to other soldiers. The one thing they never were able to take away from him, however, was his determination to survive and escape.

Preparing a close that has style and strength takes some effort. I remember in my early days as a newspaper reporter I once asked a senior editor why the number thirty was used as a code for "the end" in journalism.

"Because," he said, "I usually have to make you reporters do thirty rewrites before you come up with a decent close."

With that he handed back my article and had me rewrite the close. Amen.

PROOFREADING TECHNIQUES

Once you have finished writing and typing your feature, your work will still not be over. Next you must proofread the manuscript to ensure that it will be flawless when it is sent to the editor or publisher. Failure to proofread carefully can have devastating effects on your manuscript's sales potential. Even computer-assisted spell checkers cannot know if you meant *I, aye,* or *eye* in any given instance.

I know of one freelance writer whose entire thirty-five-hundred-word article on food preparation techniques was rejected because the author spelled *ptomaine* without the letter *p.* A costly error. (The editor figured that if the writer didn't bother to double-check spelling, she might not have bothered to check the other facts in her article. If so, it was too risky to publish it.)

I also know of a writer who accidentally typed ½ *cup* instead of ¼ *cup* in a recipe article. She was responsible for more than a thousand ruined cakes prepared by readers of the magazine her article appeared in. The editor received hundreds of complaint letters and dozens of subscription cancellations. Needless to say, that writer no longer has a working relationship with that magazine.

Writers *must* be careful proofreaders. Fortunately, proofreading isn't difficult to master. The benefits it offers in saved time and money make it worth your efforts. Let's quickly review eight tips on how to be more effective at proofreading.

Read Aloud

Reading something audibly helps you gauge its rhythm, pace, sound, and degree of difficulty. If you discover that certain passages cause you to be tongue-tied or long-winded, rewrite them more simply.

Read Backward

Some authors like to dictate rough drafts into a tape recorder. Others like to write everything out in longhand before typing it. Later, when the transcribed copy is read in the same sequence it was dictated or written out, the author often reads into the sentences things that really aren't there.

You may have this problem. Since you already know what your story or article is supposed to say, you may anticipate ("ghost") words or punctuation. To guarantee that you *do* see each word and all punctuation, try reading backward from the last word on a page to the first. By doing so, you will notice if a word is misspelled or a period has been forgotten after an abbreviation or a capital letter has been overlooked.

Use a Line Screen

An alternative to reading backward word by word is to use a five-by-seven-inch index card with a window cut one-fourth-inch wide near its top. Simply place the card's window opening over one line of type at a time. By rapidly moving up the page from the bottom line to the top, you will not be mentally caught up in any sequence of sentencing. You can critique each line for grammar, spelling, and punctuation as it appears before you.

Let It Rest

If possible, let your typed drafts or page proofs rest in a desk drawer or on your hard drive or disk for a few days. Later, you can proofread the copy with "new eyes." You will have forgotten the exact sequence you originally used in the written presentation and will now be able to judge it as an outside reader.

Juxtapose Pages

As long as the pages of a twenty-page short story are numbered, there's no reason you can't shuffle them. Each page can then be analyzed as one unit and you won't be distracted by your concentration on the overall content. Looking at the material with "new eyes" will help you catch additional problems.

Vary the Routine

If you find your desk burdened with galleys from your latest book, typed draft copy for your next book, and a final draft version of an article you have just completed, don't blitz through everything in rapid succession. Break it up. Read and approve the article and then relax and glance through your morning's mail. Read and critique the latest chapters in galleys and then peruse a magazine. Vary the proofreading pattern. This keeps you alert and fresh for your proofreading.

Consult Outsiders

Whenever you have the slightest doubt about a rule of grammar, punctuation, syntax, or spelling, use a reference source to check it. Your desk should have a dictionary, thesaurus, and a basic grammar handbook within easy reach. Other reference volumes should be on your shelf nearby. One of those reference books might be *Teach Yourself Grammar and Style in 24 Hours* by Dennis E. Hensley and Pamela Rice Hahn (Macmillan, 2000).

Assign Helpers

If you are absolutely too busy to see to it personally that your manuscripts are carefully proofread before they are sent to editors, or if you feel that you're not the best person for the task, hire a professional proofreader or rely on someone from your writers' club to help you. When you think *professional,* you don't have to think *expensive.* Some of the least expensive and most competent proofreaders are people who run freelance typing services out of their homes.

To these tips you can add others (such as always doing your own word processing to *ensure* accuracy). These eight basic points, however, are all you really need to master to ensure that your manuscripts will praise, not bury, you. Just remember that the proof is not in the pudding, it's in the reading.

AN OUTLINE ON HOW TO OUTLINE YOUR ARTICLE

We covered some of the basic issues in this chapter, but never really went into a discussion of writing the actual text of the article from beginning to end. What I've done here is given you step-by-step basics in outline form for creating your own outline and article. This outline, along with other writing helps in the chapter, should get you well on your way. If you still consider yourself a beginning writer, you can use this outline as a blueprint to follow in preparing your articles. If you have already written some articles but they have not been successful, use this outline as a checklist to determine if you have any "holes" or weaknesses in what you have written.

I. Organize and Outline the Material.

A. Make an initial content selection.

1. Decide what your purpose is in writing the piece.
2. Select a working (temporary) title.
3. Define your reading audience.
4. Determine the scope (limitations) of the piece.
5. Make a list of potential topics to be covered.

B. Do background reading and legwork research.

1. Make notes of your personal experience.
2. Interview experts in this field.
3. Read current books, pamphlets, and brochures on the topic.

C. Prepare a skeletal outline for the feature.

1. Focus on the key points (no tangents).
2. Arrange the topics in a logical sequence.

II. Write the First Draft.

A. Prepare a lead that grabs the reader's attention.

1. A shocking statement
2. Powerful descriptive scenes
3. Clever use of quotation
4. A direct statement to the reader

B. Make each word count.

1. Use short words whenever possible.
2. Use familiar (not offbeat) words.
3. Use action verbs and visual nouns.
4. Put emphasis words at the beginning or end of your sentences.
5. Master the simple declarative sentence.

C. Communicate effectively.

1. Use short paragraphs.
2. Develop good transitions between paragraphs.

3. Introduce new ideas with a topic sentence.

4. Conclude discussions with a summary statement.

5. Whenever possible, use the active voice.

6. Vary the lengths of your sentences.

III. Revise and Proofread Your Article.

A. Do a careful job of self-editing.

1. Double-check spelling, punctuation, and grammar.

2. Eliminate clichés, jargon, or libelous statements.

3. Watch out for misused words.

4. Catch any minor discrepancies in character or plot.

B. Ask yourself if the article accomplishes what you want it to.

1. Does it use anecdotes, facts, humor, pathos?

2. Does it speak to and involve the reader?

3. Does it have a coherent point of view?

4. Is the article applicable to the times and quotable?

5. Have you used effective subtitles to break up the reading?

6. Does the article offer a unique approach to the topic?

7. Are you proud to put your byline on what you have written?

CHAPTER SIX

Journalistic Techniques for Writing Nonfiction

Many famous freelance writers—Mark Twain, Ernest Hemingway, Damon Runyon, James Thurber, Stephen Crane, Jack London, Margaret Mitchell, Erskine Caldwell—began their careers as newspaper reporters. The skills they developed in such journalistic procedures as copyediting, interviewing, writing editorials, and researching topics were later useful to them in their freelance writing careers. For that reason (and others, which I'll explain as we go) we are going to take time now to discuss some of the basic techniques of research and writing that journalists use.

In our previous chapter we ended by stressing the importance of being a careful proofreader. This was to show that not everything in a first draft is worthy of publication. We now will discover, however, that even though a journalist may temporarily delete certain lines of copy, perhaps even whole paragraphs and pages, she seldom discards any of this material. Let's see how a working journalist makes maximum use of all finished writing.

FIRST AND SUBSEQUENT DRAFTS

As you get more and more adept at editing your work, you will find yourself being harsher and harsher on your material, deleting much of what you've written. Just make sure you don't overdo it.

It's good to edit your material carefully and to delete any inappropriate passages, but it's foolish to throw away any piece of fine writing. There is a very good chance you may be able to use it somewhere else sometime. As an example of this, let me tell you a true incident from literary history that may surprise you.

Most people have read Jack London's classic short story, "To Build a Fire." It's included in most high-school and college literature books. The story was published in *Century* magazine in 1908 and has since been reprinted many other places. It relates the shocking tale of a Yukon prospector who freezes to death after slipping through ice. The man's numb hands are unable to build a fire. The story is compelling, graphic, and haunting. It's a genuine masterpiece of short fiction.

But guess what? That masterpiece had its foundation in the discarded scraps of an earlier London story. Unknown to most people, Jack London published a different story called "To Build a Fire" in *Youth's Companion* on May 29, 1902. This version was shorter and less sophisticated, and in it the prospector did not freeze to death. London had been told that stories with sad endings would not sell, so he cut all harsh scenes from the first version and marketed it as a children's story. *But he held on to his original ideas.* Then, a few years later, as an established author, he wrote the version of the story he had really wanted to write. It proved to be a stunning piece of writing.

Now, how about you? What have you ever thrown away that might instead have been turned into a masterpiece? Makes you wonder, doesn't it?

Knowing what actually should be discarded and what should be saved is not always easy. Most active writers have learned to be disciplined at self-editing. It takes practice, but it can be mastered in fairly short order. There are only a few procedures to follow. Some of this was covered in the previous chapter, but I want to develop the theme of self-editing here, as it's essential for every good writer.

- Delete any off-track or tangent passages.
- Make sure all transitions are smooth.
- Double-check spelling, grammar, and typing.
- Rewrite any scenes or passages of dialogue that are predictable.
- Read the story aloud to test for pace and continuity.
- Make sure that all copy either moves the action forward or provides essential information.

Famed editor Maxwell Perkins wrote to Morley Callaghan in 1931, "When one writes a story he does not put everything in, but selects with a view to the motive of the story. The details he uses are those which are significant in the light of the motive."

Most writers know this. That's why they aren't afraid to cut. That's essential to self-editing.

But as good as they are at cutting, most writers are quite inept at salvaging good copy. Most haven't the slightest idea of what to do with an extra scene or with two pages of unused dialogue or three paragraphs of superfluous statistical research. The answer is to employ the five *R*s: retain, reslant, revise, review, and resell.

Retain

Retain everything you've had to cut. Hold it in a folder or on a disk for at least six months. Read it from time to time to keep your subconscious mind aware of it. As ideas pop up for possible uses of the salvaged segments, make notes to yourself about them on the cover of the folder or on your disk.

Reslant

As you brainstorm, ask yourself how a reslanting of the original article, along with the insertion of written segments you previously cut, might help create a new article. For example, if your first version was geared toward men, perhaps your new version could be slanted toward women readers. If the previous version was for juveniles, maybe the new version could be made to appeal to senior citizens.

Another way to reslant the article is to take something you previously deleted and use it as your new perspective. For example, your first version may have focused on *people* who design and make quilts. To keep the article on track, you deleted all paragraphs that explained how to make quilts. Now, however, in your new version, you could slant the article toward a *how-to* format and use data about people simply as filler or local color for your new article.

You can go right through standard journalistic procedures in reslanting an article. The first article could emphasize the "who" of the topic; the second article could emphasize the "what"; the third article the "when" (and so on until you've also covered "where, why, how, and how much"). This gives you seven totally different slants and enables you to make use of virtually every scrap of previously deleted copy.

Revise

Revising an article can also create new openings for unused copy. Pull out your first draft and go back through it. Delete 25 percent of what you have written. For a 3,000-word feature, you will have to cut 750 words; usually you will cut general background information, certain descriptive passages, and perhaps some dialogue. Now, insert 750 words of previously unpublished copy about the topic. Give your article a new lead, some quotations from different people, and a few interesting statistics. With these brushstrokes, you will have a new article.

Another method of revision is to bring your article up to date. Contact your previous sources and ask about new developments, the latest statistics and facts, new quotations, new predictions, new views, new circumstances. Take these new elements, combine them with material you previously had no room for in the original version, and write a new article about something that is old hat to you.

Another revision procedure is to organize all of your deleted passages that deal with sensory elements and use them to have the reader experience the topic. Instead of an impersonal report on the topic, offer a vivid presentation of the sounds, smells, tastes, sights, and tactile sensations associated with skydiving or Christmas caroling or garden planting or whatever else your topic may be. You will be basing everything on all your original research, but your writing will be completely new and innovative.

A final revision tip is to give your first draft to another writer or editor and ask, "How do you think this could have been better?" When the responses come back—"More words from expert sources" or "The old mansion should have been described more clearly" or "It needs some humor"—you then can go to your folder or disk of "cut" passages and pull out whatever is needed.

Review

After numerous reslantings and revisions of your original article, your file folder will soon be bulging. It then will be time to review carefully all of your material. As you review, ask yourself these questions:

1. Do I now have enough material on this topic to form the basis of a book, pamphlet, or lecture series that could generate extra income for me?
2. Could I rewrite my material for a different medium, such as a business training film (screenplay) or a cassette tape series (audio script)?

Resell

If your review leads you to believe there is a potential afterlife in a new medium for your published articles (lectures, films, tapes, books), develop a proposal, contact an editor, and resell your material. And as you begin revising for the new markets, don't throw away anything you cut. Remember, it's all grist for the next trip to the mill.

WRITING EDITORIALS

At this point you may be convinced that you understand all the procedures for writing a good article. Nevertheless, you may wish that there was a training ground where you could practice your skills awhile before sending a freelance article or query letter to a magazine. Well, there is such a place: the letters page of your specialty magazine and the editorial page of your local newspaper.

One of the benefits of living in a society that permits freedom of speech and of the press is the chance it gives you to sound off about matters that really irritate or please you. One of the most effective ways of doing this is by writing a guest editorial for your local newspaper or a specialty magazine. Not only do you get the satisfaction of having your views put before the public, but many times a cash payment is also given to freelance editorialists.

Editorials deal with very current, often fleeting, issues. They are brief, and they deal with contemporary topics and examples. They are not meant to be lasting items of literature.

Most editorials set out to do one of four things: support a stance or action, disagree with an issue, laud something or someone, or educate the public about a matter. Your objective in writing the editorial will be to woo people into reading what you have to say, to help them comprehend your views, and then to convince them that your position is valid.

Good editorials will have a natural zest. The copy will challenge, awaken, entertain, inform, interpret, and/or guide the reader. The readers of editorials are looking for reflective thinking, additional data on a subject, and a clear interpretation of the meaning and significance of the issue under consideration.

Basically, there are seventeen generic topics that editorials focus on and deal with. They are: values, trends, culture, patriotism, education, rights, science, business, technology, politics, laws, people, history, economics, health, religion, and art.

The format for the short editorial used primarily in newspapers is as follows:

- title
- news peg noted
- personal opinion stated
- rationale explained

Such editorials range from three to ten paragraphs. They usually use a standard news peg to note the event, such as "Last Tuesday, Mayor Jones announced…" or "In a recent congressional session, a motion was made to…" Having summarized the item of conversation, the writer then offers an opinion on the matter. The transition into this phase may begin, "The danger in this action is…" or "Another side to this issue is…" or something similar. Having stated an opinion, the writer then justifies it with quotes or statistics or lessons from history or similar documentation.

Magazine editorials allow more space for reflection and analysis. They follow a longer format along these lines:

- title
- announcement of topic
- summation of general opinions on the subject
- agreement with reaction to those opinions
- justification of writer's views
- close/challenge to readers

This magazine format allows for a more detailed overview of the subject, a more intensive case for or against the issue, and greater support of the writer's claim.

Every person who begins to read any kind of newspaper or magazine article will proceed from one paragraph to the next wondering, *How does this relate to me?* The editorial writer answers that most basic question by saying, "This is *how, why,* and *when* this type of news relates to you. Furthermore, this is how I feel you should react to it." That's what makes a good editorial. Since you undoubtedly have some set opinions about things, you will have a chance to practice your writing, share your views, and gain byline exposure without having to do a lot of extra research. This is just one more way in which journalism training can enhance your overall skills in nonfiction writing.

CONDUCTING INTERVIEWS

Once you have gained some experience as an editorial writer, the next step in your writing development plan should be to master interviewing. All writers must become good interviewers. Let me explain why.

Nonfiction writers cannot write contemporary biographies unless they know thoroughly how to interview the people they wish to profile—and also those people who are close to the person being profiled. Furthermore, you need to enrich your feature articles with quotations in order to hold a reader's interest, and that means you must obtain quotes through interviews. Even facts for straight works of journalism are often gathered through interviews with researchers, eyewitnesses, civic leaders, or corporate executives. Similarly, the journalist's approach to the interview also helps the fiction writer, who cannot create a sense of verisimilitude (realism and believability) unless she has become very familiar with a novel or short story's locale, time period, people, and general background. This often requires long interview sessions with people who are closely related to the topic. For example, before he wrote his novel *Airport,* Arthur Hailey worked two months as a baggage carrier, flight steward, ticket counter assistant, pilot's aide, and control tower observer. All the while, he watched his colleagues at work, questioned them continually about their lives and jobs, and took photos of them performing their duties. He then knew each job and each person well enough to sit down and work them into the plot of a best-selling novel. Years later Michael Crichton did equal amounts of research before he wrote his novel *Airframe,* also about the airline industry.

The interviewer's basic tools include two ink pens, two pencils, a notepad, a camera, film, a cassette recorder, three blank tapes, a spare microphone, extra batteries, and a long list of questions. (When buying a microcassette recorder for interviews, buy one that has an automatic shutoff when the tape comes to an end on each side. Otherwise, you'll continue to interview but none of it will be recorded.)

When preparing for the interview, always work with Murphy's Law ("If it *can* go wrong, it *will* go wrong") and be prepared in advance in case your pen goes dry, your microphone cord develops a short, or your cassette tape gets tangled and breaks.

Prior to the interview, learn as much as you can about your subject. Put together a folder on the person. Fill it with other articles written about him or her, any profile material provided by a press agent or company public relations worker, or anything the subject has written (even if for a trade journal or professional publication).

Show up a little early for the interview so that you don't keep the person waiting and so that you can spend a few moments asking related questions of a secretary or spouse. Try to conduct the interview at the interviewee's home or office. Be sure to dress in an appropriate manner: men should wear dress shirts, ties, and sport coats or suits when in formal situations, such as interviewing professors or bank executives, but dress more casually if in a sports locker room or talking to teenagers. Women should wear skirts and blouses or suits for more formal meetings, but slacks or more casual attire for less formal interviews. Be an effective listener when you interview. Use good body language, keep your mind on the topic at hand, and observe common courtesy (don't interrupt people when they are talking, don't "talk along" with people, and don't try to put words in people's mouths). Ask one question at a time (no five-parters).

Don't ask your questions so slowly that your interviewee gets bored; but do start slowly enough so that the person does not feel intimidated. Don't try to find out everything; just focus on one or two main areas. Strive for the person's thoughts, feelings, ideas, opinions, and views rather than facts you can look up somewhere else. Save your toughest questions for last.

Prepare your questions in a logical order: "What kind of reading do you enjoy?" should be followed by, "What was the last book you read?" since the two questions are linked thematically. Begin with a discussion of the basics: parents, childhood, schools, military service, family life. Be specific when discussing career aspects: promotions, titles, responsibilities, achievements, current projects. Touch generally on leisure activities: hobbies, sports, travel, clubs.

Let your tape recorder "worry" about capturing the person's words. You will use your notepad to fill in details about the atmosphere: the interviewee's appearance, tone of voice, stance, walk, gestures, clothes, office or home decor, height, coloring, weight.

Don't wait too long after an interview to write it. It's best to prepare your manuscript while things are fresh in your mind. Decide which format your receiving publications would prefer: questions and answers, a profile feature, or a first-person narrative. Let the person talk throughout your interview—50 percent direct quotations, 50 percent related information—and tell his or her own story. Whenever possible, use humor, irony, satirical developments, or surprising remarks to keep your copy lively.

QUOTING EXPERTS

Part of the appeal of an interview, aside from the fact that people enjoy reading about famous personalities, is that interviews often provide free advice and consultation. That's why interviewing is so important. People want the opinions of experts.

In 50 B.C. the Roman poet Virgil wrote, "Believe a person who has proved it himself. Believe an expert." People do believe experts. Knowing this, freelance writers can double or triple their chances of selling articles by making it a point to quote experts. Let's face it. Whose opinion on Toyota automobiles carries more weight with you, a guy who owns one Toyota or a mechanic who has worked on nine hundred Toyotas? Get the point?

Whether or not you are aware of it, you are already in the habit of citing expert sources all the time. In your conversations you are frequently apt to say things like, "I've got this friend in real estate who tells me..." or "As my grandfather used to say..." By bringing in the expertise of an outside person, you give your story more believability and authenticity. The same thing applies to article writing.

Besides authenticity, however, quotes from experts give your article more depth, a greater variety of opinions, and a break from the monotony of just presenting your own words. Put into a sidebar, they can even provide a format variation for your article.

Finding experts on given topics is not difficult. Very few experts are known to people, so any individuals with appropriate credentials, such as your pastor, your family physician, or your college professors, can serve as expert sources.

You can give your article more national appeal by citing sources outside your local sphere. There are several ways to go about this.

Tape-Record Radio and TV Interviews

You may quote from someone else's interview as long as you don't seriously diminish the value of the original program by borrowing too heavily. Remember to cite your reference (interviewer, interviewee, show, station or network, and date).

Quote from Original Articles and Books Written by Experts

This is perfectly legal, especially if you quote fewer than 250 words. For courtesy's sake, most writers will send a letter to the publisher seeking permission to quote from a book. It is seldom denied (most writers and publishers are grateful for the publicity) but may take weeks or months to receive.

Read and Quote

Read specialty periodicals and organizational publications and quote the publications themselves. There is nothing wrong with saying, "A Harris poll cited in *Newsweek* on July 19th showed that…" or "According to an editorial in the *Saturday Evening Post* in May of this year.…"

Conduct Mail Interviews with Experts

Send a form letter to eight or ten experts on the topic you plan to write about. With the letter, attach a page of five to fifteen questions and enclose a stamped, self-addressed envelope. Usually, only three out of ten will take the time to respond, but three experts are all you need. There are also a variety of on-line resources, such as ProfNet *(www.profnet.com),* that will link you to experts in various fields of research.

Call the Places Where the Experts Work

You can contact the public relations or publicity directors of universities, businesses, and organizations and ask for an interview appointment with someone who is an expert on your topic or area of interest. Hospitals, fraternal organizations, and political parties also have helpful PR people who can arrange for you to interview key people. Tell them you want to talk to someone with a substantial track record in that area of interest and who is currently on the cutting edge in knowledge, research, and production.

Conduct Phone Interviews

The phone interview is probably the best of these techniques. (Remember, long-distance phone calls related to article research are tax-deductible, and e-mail interviews are often free.)

A long-distance interview gives your hometown articles national scope. Begin by going to the *Readers' Guide to Periodical Literature* in the reference section of your local library. Look up articles written about your topic during the past five years. Locate copies of these articles, read them, and make a note of the authors and the experts cited. Find their phone numbers by dialing information.

When you phone an expert, explain what your topic is, which publication you plan to market the article to, and why you feel the person you are talking to would make a good resource person. Ask when it would be convenient for you to call back to talk for thirty minutes. Set up a specific appointment. If the phone call is not convenient, ask if you can submit questions on e-mail for the expert to respond to.

In the interim, read all you can by and about the expert you will be interviewing. Prepare a long list of questions. Since your article will probably cite at least three experts, you may want each expert to focus intently on different sets of questions related to your topic.

When you make your follow-up call, remember to inform the expert that you are taping the interview. You can purchase a suction-cup microphone attachment for your phone that is linked to a cord running to your tape recorder. This will record everything spoken on the phone during the conversation. Also, ask the individual to send a recent personal photo to you, along with permission for its use and the name of the photographer. As you talk, try to get the expert's views, ideas, feelings, and predictions about the topic rather than just statistics. The facts you do need to get, however, should be checked for accuracy at the end of the interview (spelling of names and places, dates, and so on). Keep a notepad in front of you to supplement the tape recorder and to note any hesitancies, reactions, drawls, or other attention-arresting factors.

When you transcribe your tapes for your article, feel free to exercise poetic license in correcting a person's grammar and in condensing the person's sentences, as long as the meaning stays the same. For example, the tape recording may have, "Let's see, I, uh, came out here around—oh, what was it?—around 1998…June, now that I think of it." That quote can be written in your article as, "I came here in June of 1998."

To help the reader "see" the expert, you may wish to add a few descriptive or scene-setting words, such as "Dr. Schutt paused, cleared his throat, then replied, 'Of course, back then we had no idea that cyclamates could cause cancer.'"

You can keep your list of experts loyal to you by sending each one a copy of the published article that mentions them. (This is the *only* pay any expert should expect to receive for time and services.)

There is something in all readers that makes us want to get advice from experts, especially if we don't have to pay a high consulting fee. If your articles can offer such free advice, *you* will become an *expert* on manuscript sales.

HOW TO WRITE FOR RELIGIOUS PERIODICALS

Here are my suggestions for writing for religious periodicals. This is a great market for freelancers.

- Offer a religious slant—but don't overindulge in theology on every page; for example, an article on business ethics could be supported by pertinent Bible verses, or a feature on stress management could include references to prayer and meditation.

- Provide pragmatic, useful information for the reader.
- Try to avoid "churchology" vocabulary (e.g., *born again, glory hallelujah,* etc.) unless it is a general term (e.g., *tithe, stewardship, witness*).
- Don't try to write for Christians unless you are one. If you are not intimate with Christian spirituality you may end up trying to tack "something religious" onto the end of your articles instead of knowing how to weave it naturally into the body of the writing.
- Remember that Christian readers expect a solution to a problem to come about by combining divine intervention (through prayer, Bible reading, or other means) with practical applications (which are based on biblical tenets).
- Most Christian nonfiction books or lesson-oriented articles are written in the first person because most of them are providing counseling, teaching, or first-person experiences.
- Never try to write about something you either haven't been directly involved in yourself or haven't spent adequate time researching. The only exception to this rule comes in writing an "as told to" book or article, in which you would be organizing and presenting information from a "name" author.
- Don't try to bend Scripture verses to fit some topic you are writing about. Taking verses out of context will upset readers and editors. If what you are writing about has no Bible reference (auto repair, skydiving), just present it in a straightforward manner.
- Nonfiction articles in the Christian field are usually one thousand to twenty-five hundred words long. The tone should be upbeat yet familiar, like a pleasant visit with a lively friend. Anecdotes, dialogue, and good descriptions appeal to editors and readers.
- Never assume that rules of professionalism don't apply simply because some religious-oriented publications pay slightly less than some secular publications do. Everything from proper manuscript format to meticulous research applies in this field, too.
- Scan your newspaper to find topics of a controversial nature—gun control, genetic engineering, euthanasia—that you can research and respond to from a Christian perspective. Suggestions include human

values, religious versus secular schools, TV evangelism, Christian politicians, abortion, business ethics, and drug abuse.

- Editors eagerly want people-oriented articles. Personal dramas, interviews, uplifting incidents, real-life personal accounts, celebrity profiles, and historical biographical sketches are all popular in Christian periodicals.

WHAT ABOUT PHOTOGRAPHY?

Before we leave the subject of article writing, we need to discuss some points about photography. Although it is not the intention of this book to discuss anything other than writing, the fact remains that more than 75 percent of all freelance article manuscripts must be accompanied by visual art (photos, slides, cartoons, maps, or drawings) or else they will appear inadequate to the recipient editor.

If you prefer not to do photography, check with the public relations department of a school or business associated with your topic. See if they can provide photos. You can also hire as freelancers high-school or college students who do photography for campus newspapers.

If you want to try your own photography, don't be intimidated. Most cameras today provide light adjustment and automatic focus features. Here are fourteen tips on how to handle your own photography.

1. When photographing, don't be afraid to move, direct, and impose upon your subjects in order to set up the type of picture you want to take.
2. Shoot plenty of photos, but change the settings so that your photo essay does not seem redundant. Capture different views, different rooms, and different people.
3. Avoid artificial lighting, whenever possible. Try to make your photos seem real, not stiff, posed, or unnatural.
4. Take a picture of anything that strikes you as interesting; make both a horizontal and a vertical shot of it if time and film permit.
5. Move closer, not farther away, on most shots. Pictures taken from far away show too much background and clutter.

6. Make the setting of your photos appropriate to the person you are writing your article about. Shoot a tennis pro on the courts, a business executive in a business office, a service station attendant with the station in the background.

7. Only include mood shots or experimental photography (blurred images, fish-eyed lenses) after you have sent an editor plenty of straight, standard journalistic photos.

8. Have a rubber stamp made with your name and address on it and a mention of the rights you are selling to your photographs. Stamp this information on the back of each of the photos you submit to an editor.

9. When mailing photos, place them between two pieces of sturdy cardboard and send them in an envelope you have clearly marked: "PHOTOGRAPHS: Do Not Bend."

10. Get yourself a paraphernalia bag to carry along on assignments. Inside it put your notepads, extra rolls of film, pencils and pens, spare lenses, and other needed items of equipment or extras. You may even want to include a disposable camera as a backup unit.

11. Use a model's release form for subjects you feel may later regret they posed for photos. In some instances, it might even be safer to have everyone sign the form. Always have your photo subject sign a model's release form when putting someone into a photograph that will be used to endorse something or someone (such as a political candidate). I've included a sample model's release form at the end of this chapter. Journalistic ethics require that you limit the use of the photos taken for one story to that particular story or very similar stories. It would be wrong to take photos under the pretense of writing about someone's style of decorating a home and then use those photos in a different article about stay-at-home moms.

12. When writing captions for your photos, provide all the necessary information. Your captions should identify everyone in the picture, tell when it was taken, where it was taken, and have all people and place names spelled correctly.

13. Keep your negatives. Start a subject/index file so that you can get at the photos you need without any delay or trouble.

14. Be familiar with the copyright laws as they apply to photographs. You can check the annual issue of *Photographer's Market* for information on laws or call the Copyright Office's hotline: (202) 287-9100.

Photojournalists used to use 35-mm cameras almost exclusively. The *mm* refers to millimeters, and 35 mm is the film size. If you want a versatile camera, you must be willing to pay between $250 and $475 for it. Remember, this cost is tax-deductible. More and more, however, digital cameras are making life easier for journalists who work on computer and the Internet. These cameras use computer disks, not film, to record their images. Formerly very expensive, these are coming down in price and can be much more versatile. They allow you to send an image over the Internet or place it in your article yourself. Look for magazine articles such as those in *Consumer Reports* to sort out the best camera and features for your needs. With photography under your belt and good nonfiction writing skills, you will be ready to sell your articles widely.

The last two chapters have carefully reviewed the procedures for developing such salesworthy articles. Now we will switch our attention to the study of fiction writing. The next chapter will explain the ways in which fiction and nonfiction writing are similar and the ways in which they differ. If you have never tried your hand at fiction writing, chapter seven will show you how you can quickly develop ideas and writing procedures that will help you break into this field.

Sample Model's Release Form

In consideration for value received, receipt whereof acknowledged, I hereby give *(name of freelance photographer)* the absolute right and permission to copyright and/or publish, and/or resell photographic portraits or pictures of me, or in which I may be included in whole or in part, for art, advertising, trade, or any other lawful purpose whatsoever.

I hereby waive any right that I may have to inspect and/or approve the finished product or the advertising copy that may be used in connection therewith, or the use to which it may be applied.

I hereby release, discharge, and agree to save *(the accepting publication or the writer's name)* from any liability by virtue of any blurring, distortion, alteration, optical illusion, or use in composite form, whether intentional or otherwise, that may occur or be produced in the making of said pictures, or in any processing tending toward the completion of the finished product.

Date _____ Model _____

Address _____

_____

Witness _____

Writing Quality Fiction

Most of the rules and guidelines that apply to nonfiction writing also apply to fiction writing—excellence in grammar, syntax, and vocabulary, as well as the need for good leads and closings. But there are additional lessons that apply *only* to fiction. This is particularly true if you intend to write long works of fiction, such as novels.

In this chapter I would like to focus on how many fiction writers go about developing characters and plots for their short stories. In the earliest years of my career as a writer, I wrote a steady stream of short stories for such Sunday-school papers and regional magazines as *Conquest, Challenge, War Cry, Young Ambassador,* and *Purpose.* It not only gave me byline exposure and pocket money, it helped me learn to pay attention to the unique characteristics all people have. It also taught me that daily dramas in a person's life are the "stuff" of good works of fiction.

Many times, a writer's ethics and beliefs can be explained in more understandable ways when placed within the context of a fictional work. John Bunyan's *Pilgrim's Progress,* though an adventure allegory, explained the challenges a person of religious faith must face during his or her earthly life. John Milton's *Paradise Lost* was a dramatic explanation of the heavenly battle between God and Satan.

More contemporary writers such as C. S. Lewis, J. R. R. Tolkien, Catherine Marshall, Jerry Jenkins, and Janette Oke have proved that an ethical and healing message can be shared in every genre of fiction, whether fantasy or love story, detective mystery or historical romance. Many people who would never darken a church door or go to a counseling center would have no qualms about reading a good novel recommended to them by a friend. Fiction often provides readers a look at various spiritual and psychological dimensions at work in the lives of people, and fiction often presents these ideas in nonthreatening ways to the general reader. With such promising new ways of reaching people with a spiritual message, let's now examine some specific procedures you can follow in learning to write quality fiction. We will look first at how to develop main characters.

DEVELOPING FICTIONAL CHARACTERS

F. Scott Fitzgerald once said, "An author ought to write for the youth of his own generation, the critics of the next, and the schoolmasters of ever afterward."

The trick to mastering Fitzgerald's ambition seems to be in developing unforgettable fictional characters. The reason characters such as Jo March, Captain Ahab, Hester Prynne, Ebenezer Scrooge, Don Quixote, Huckleberry Finn, and Scarlett O'Hara fascinate readers and stand the test of time is because they are distinct, three-dimensional, vibrant personalities. They were purposely created by their authors to live forever. And thus far they have.

If readers are not fascinated by fictional characters, they will not care what happens to them; and if they don't care what happens to them, they will put down the story about them. So, your characters need to be interesting, amusing, vivid, and challenging.

As the author, *you* must know your characters better than anyone else. Particularly in writing a novel, you should prepare a dossier on each one, with as much depth and information recorded there as you would have if you were researching a real person's life before writing his or her biography. In developing your fictional characters, keep the following seven points in mind:

Originality. Your character must be original and not a fictional portrait of your Aunt Molly or favorite school teacher. Characters are created to fit the plot, not to pay token homage to some real individual. This is true even when the characters are actually modeled after real people. For example, Jonas Cord in *The Carpetbaggers* is modeled after the late billionaire Howard Hughes, but the two also have many, many differences.

Challenge. Your character must *try to solve his or her own problem,* since that is what makes the plot tension in your story. In *For Whom the Bell Tolls,* no one could blow the bridge except Robert Jordan, since he was the only explosives expert. In *The Time Machine,* no one could go into the future in the one-seated machine except its inventor.

Motivation. Your characters must *be motivated by something,* so that whatever they create or solve or change or steal or fight against to their last ounce of strength will seem logical in the context of the story. Scarlett O'Hara's love for Tara makes her fight to hold on to the land even in war. Captain Ahab's insane passion to find and kill Moby Dick is fueled by the revenge he seeks against the whale for having bitten off his leg. Phileas Fogg's mania to go around the world in eighty days is fostered by the desire he has to get even with the men at his club who laughed at him for even *thinking* that such a stunt was possible. The dog Buck's need to answer the call of the wild is fanned by his natural instincts to be free, wild, and cunning. All fictional characters must have a believable motivation for their actions.

Distinction. All characters must *have distinctive traits,* some good and some bad. No one is perfect. That's the reality of being human—and keeping your characters real and human is the key to good fiction. As frugal and bitter as Scrooge was, he still had elements of basic honesty. As brave and courageous as Oedipus was, he still had elements of self-pride and arrogance. As daring and fearless as Indiana Jones seemed to be, he was still terrified of snakes. Fictional characters must be as balanced as real people.

Consistency. Characters also must *be consistent,* so that they do not talk or walk or act differently in one chapter than they do in the previous one. The female who is a blonde in chapter two should not be a redhead in chapter seven. The lawyer with the New England accent in chapter one should not have a Southern drawl by the end of the book.

Independence. All characters must *be allowed lives of their own,* so that if they suddenly start going in some unexpected direction as you are writing, you will let them go there if it seems natural. Not even *you* know the depth of information stored in your subconscious mind. You may have new ideas just under the surface waiting to escape through your moving pencil or blinking cursor.

Involvement. Finally, main characters must *be involved in plot conflict. They* must find themselves pitted against people, nature, fate, or even God. It doesn't matter *what* the conflict is, so long as it's intriguing, challenging, and suspenseful. But there must be a conflict for your characters.

Now that you've got this overview on developing fictional characters, let's see how you can use the nonfiction techniques you have learned to help you develop characters for fiction.

Filling Out Your Characters' Lives

My training in newspaper reporting, magazine interviewing, and book researching has focused my career heavily on nonfiction. Nevertheless, I enjoy writing fiction, and I have discovered that my training in journalistic investigative procedures can be applied to creating believable fictional characters. Let me explain.

Whenever a news story breaks, reporters scramble to discover and report on the five *W*s and the two *H*s: *who, what, when, where, why, how,* and *how much.* However, after this surface news has been reported, feature writers are then assigned to get an in-depth understanding of the full story. For example, if the surface news is that the mayor has resigned, the feature writers will find out what impact this will have on the mayor's political party, how his or her family feels about it, who convinced the mayor to act now, how the public feels about this, and what the mayor's remaining options are for a career in politics.

Basically, the feature writer will try to make the feature story lively and intriguing first by making the profiled person seem three-dimensional and then by making the associated news event seem important and timely. This is done by answering the four following questions:

- What are the circumstances of the news event?
- What was the person's background?
- What does the person look like?
- What was the person's motive?

Good fictional characters can be developed by answering the same questions. After all, fictional characters have to *seem* real to readers. So, let's review these four questions in that light.

Placing Characters in a Plot

We know that without plot conflict (circumstances) there can be no story. So, your fictional character must be placed into a situation of stress. This is not difficult since there are only nine fundamental plot conflicts for you to choose from:

- character against himself or herself
- character against character
- character against God
- character against nature/environment
- character against predetermined fate
- character against the unknown
- character against a machine
- character against society/culture
- character against circumstances (being fired; contracting a disease; getting deserted on an island)

Having selected a generic topic, you then need only to narrow it to something specific within that range. If, for example, you select *character against machine*, you may wish to write a sad story about an elderly crossing guard who is replaced by a stoplight or write a crime story about computer experts who try to break into computerized corporate payroll systems. (The movie *Sneakers* with Robert Redford and Sidney Poitier is a good example of this.) The options and variations are limitless.

Creating a Detailed Description

Next, you need to fabricate a detailed dossier on your main characters. Here are some questions to ask:

1. Where was he or she born, educated, employed?
2. Which parent, sibling, teacher, friend, or relative had a major influence on this person?
3. What political party, religious affiliation, military service branch, and/or labor union has this person belonged to?

4. What does the person look like? What are his or her personal habits?

Although detailing these facts is a bit time consuming, it's much quicker than having to dig up all these facts about a real person. Besides, it's fun. You get to create a person from scratch.

The dossier gives you a permanent record of each of your characters so that each person is consistent in looks and behavior throughout your work of fiction. Each dossier also helps you delineate your characters by purposely not making them all redheads or all twenty-year-old college students or ex-Marines.

I have a personality profile sheet (see special section at chapter end) that I use as a research guide whenever I am hired to do a magazine profile of someone. I use this same sheet whenever I am creating a fictional character.

Naturally, only about one-tenth of the information in the profile will ever get mentioned in your story. That is not important. What is important is that you know your character thoroughly so that your character will be realistic. What *does* get mentioned about your character truly will be important for the reader to know.

Further, you need to "see" what your character looks like. Whenever I am getting ready to interview a famous person, I obtain several pictures of that person from magazines, PR agents, or high-school or college yearbooks. I study the eyes, the expressions, even the posture in order to give me a sense of the person.

You should complete a profile for each of your major fictional characters and perhaps create a shortened version for your minor characters. Then, carefully review the facts in your dossiers and, as you do, thumb through magazines, mail-order catalogs, brochures, and pamphlets until you find pictures of models or actors or other people who are flesh-and-blood manifestations of your fictional characters.

Cut out these pictures and mount them on a character board (bulletin board) across from your writing desk. Put the character's name in bold letters below the picture. Now your characters not only have histories, they also have faces. They are real, at least to you and your readers. The more you look at your characters, the more lifelike they will seem to you. In character development, seeing does lead to believing, knowing, and creating.

Developing Your Characters' Motives

Your final step is to develop motives for what your characters will be doing. In an investigative journalism assignment, if I am trying to figure out why a real-life person behaved the way he did, I go back to the data I have obtained for the personality profile. Then I ask myself, *Why did this man abuse his wife?* According to my research I am reminded that his father had beaten his mother regularly. Perhaps the young man was conditioned to disrespect spouses? There is the possible motive: like father, like son. Not a justification for those actions, but it at least gives me a reason and understanding as to why his motive exists.

The dossiers of your fictional characters will give you similar ideas for character behavior patterns and motives. Keep in mind that your main characters have to solve their own problems, since that makes a plot.

As I mentioned earlier, your characters must be motivated by something all-consuming, such as ambition, fame, power, or revenge, so that their actions will seem logical within the context of the story. For example, you and I wouldn't have gotten into the ring against Mike Tyson at the peak of his boxing career for all the gold in Fort Knox (pure suicide). However, in a similar situation, we *do* believe that Rocky Balboa would go against Apollo Creed (a similar suicidal mission) because the author has convinced us that, win or lose, here is a guy who must at least take his shot at the championship. It's completely believable *within the context* of that story.

You must allow your characters to have that life of their own that I wrote about earlier. Let them surprise you occasionally. Once the novelist Balzac was approached at a party by an angry woman.

"Sir!" she exclaimed. "I have just finished reading your latest novel. I simply could not believe it when that beautiful eighteen-year-old princess ran off with that seventy-two-year-old baron."

"I assure you, madam," replied Balzac, "I was as shocked as you were."

All writers have a mental file cabinet filled with memories of unusual characters they have encountered in life. While not actually copying down real-life characters, if you can tap into those memories, organize them into dossiers, and find faces to match them, you will have several three-dimensional people to write about. Thereafter, it's just a matter of asking yourself, *How would this sort of person react if confronted by a dead body…or an escaped convict…or a sudden bankruptcy…or the birth of triplets…or an unexpected scholarship?*

And you will know the answers. After all, they are *your* people.

WRITING EFFECTIVE DIALOGUE

Dialogue, when used effectively, can add variety and zest to both fiction and nonfiction manuscripts. Most novelists try to keep a fifty-fifty balance between dialogue and general narrative. And most nonfiction feature writers try to make their articles "quote rich" to sustain reference credibility and to offer format variety.

Effective dialogue should *be condensed,* so that your characters say in twenty words what would take someone in real life two hundred words to say.

Dialogue should *advance the plot,* so that what is being said will give information about elements of the plot or create a new problem for the characters.

Dialogue also should *add to character development,* in that vocabulary, slang, syntax, grammar, or drawls found in dialogue should reveal a great deal about the person doing the speaking. (Slang should be used sparingly. An occasional slang term will be adequate for establishing the character's identity. Editors and readers will not tolerate twenty pages of dialogue filled with slang words such as *gonna, wanna, dunno, c'mon, whazzat,* and *lessee.*)

Most of the time, dialogue should be followed by the word *said* or by nothing at all if it is obvious who the speaker is. A few acceptable substitutes (to avoid constant repetition) are as follows: *replied, agreed, answered, whispered, asked,* or *shouted.* To imply emotion an occasional adverb can be placed near *said,* as in "he said cautiously" or "she said wistfully." Go easy on such substitutes for *said* as *proclaimed, expostulated, vociferated, enunciated, expounded,* or *broadcast.* Such words often sound overstated. Furthermore, do not write that a character "smiled" a word ("Yes," she smiled). It is impossible to smile words or to grin words or to scowl words.

In gauging and evaluating the dialogue you have created for your manuscript, read it aloud and ask yourself these questions:

- Is it void of clichés, too much slang, and trite expressions?
- Does it make the page more appealing to the reader's eye?

- Does it make it obvious as to what the character's mood is (anger, surprise, sympathy)?
- Is it condensed rather than verbose?
- Does it advance or support the main plot?
- Does it sound natural and not condescending?
- Does it reveal oddities, quirks, and characteristics about the person speaking?

One of the best ways to master dialogue is to become a student of it. Carry a pad and pen with you and record the speech patterns of various people. How does a housewife's telephone chatter differ from a minister's sermon? How does a dock worker's bark differ from a politician's speech? How does a college professor's lecture differ from a shoe retailer's pitch?

Make notes regarding speech patterns, jargon, shop talk, and delivery. Make notes regarding which speakers spoke tersely or flippantly or were soft-spoken or brash. Apply these real-life vocal attributes to your fictional characters.

Archibald MacLeish once noted, "Writers, if they are worthy of that designation, do not write for other writers. They write to give reality to experience." A key element of this reality is powerful dialogue.

CREATING PLOT TENSION

A fictional plot is created whenever an author presents something *unusual* or abnormal that, within the context of the story, is made to seem logical. For example, when Sydney Carton willingly dies in place of Charles Darnay in *A Tale of Two Cities* by Charles Dickens, it becomes believable because of the bond established between the central characters as the story progressed. But how can we determine what the something *unusual* actually is?

Establishing a hierarchy of human needs and then changing the order of several of the steps will create something unusual. I work from a seven-point hierarchical scale of factors that I believe are human priorities:

1. life
2. health
3. security (religious, monetary, societal)
4. prestige/status

5. sensual stimulation (food, sex, music)

6. mental stimulation (reading, conversation)

7. suspended action (sleep)

The next step in creating a plot is to shuffle the levels of the motivational priorities list and, thereby, to create conflict and plot. As might be presumed, the higher the priorities being dealt with, the more intriguing the story. For example, it is quite normal for a man dying of cancer to spend all of his money searching for a cure. In other words, "life" (step one) outranks "security" (step three). Now, if a story in which "security" outranks "life" can be written logically, it can have tremendous impact. A prime example is the New Testament story of Christ sacrificing his life for the spiritual security of mankind. In fact, at least one writer has called this *The Greatest Story Ever Told.* Charles Dickens, as noted earlier, also used this thematic technique in the climax of *A Tale of Two Cities,* in which Carton dies in place of Darnay.

With seven completely different categories, an infinite number of dramatic plots can be devised through continual inversion of the order of priorities.

How do you begin? Simply establish your character and begin to put him or her in fascinating and unusual circumstances. Let's create an example. Our character is a middle-aged, married physician with a good practice. To get our story started, we reverse steps five and four by having him make advances toward a young female patient; here, his romantic desires are becoming more important than his respected status in the community.

Next, we could reverse steps four and three by having the physician denounce his lifelong Catholic beliefs in order to adopt Judaism, since it is rumored that he is being considered as the next chief administrator at Mount Sinai Hospital; here, his drive for status becomes more important than the security of his long-held religious beliefs.

Third, we could reverse steps six and five. We can have our physician come in contact with a newly arrived, brilliant young surgeon who so fascinates our character that he begins to skip meals and overlook opportunities to flirt with his patient, choosing instead to discuss operating techniques with the new doctor. Here, our character's mental stimulation dominates his previous desires.

Finally, at the close of the story, we can draw things together by having the doctor experience something that helps him put his human priorities back in perspective. The scene may call for an old Protestant minister to arrive at the hospital, ailing and obviously near death. He shares his life story and faith testimony with the doctor and then dies with a contented expression on his face. This makes the doctor realize his own frailty. He wants the complete peace the old minister had. He has tried wanton morals, church jumping, and career success, yet he has never found happiness. He reaches over and removes a Bible from the dead man's hands and bows in silent prayer. At last, step one (life…eternal) outranks everything else.

And so the plotting patterns can continue, on and on, up and down the scale. This is the method of operation employed by novelists who write thousand-page books, jumping from one unusual and captivating situation to the next. Naturally, progressing up the scale increases character tension and, thereby, character interest. In reverse, going down the scale provides relief and a momentary stay of anxiety.

Unlike a short story, in plotting a novel, it is best to center the book on two dominant "main interest" characters and two or three characters of lesser importance. For balance, certain characters should be rapidly rising on the scale of conflicting motivators, while other characters are simultaneously descending the scale. In this fashion, there is always some element of relief for the reader and some element of suspense.

The more radical the shift in positions on the scale, the more intriguing the story becomes. By shifting step four above step two, we can intensify the plot considerably. This sort of play can be found in a story wherein a soldier during the Spanish-American War volunteers under medical supervision to let mosquitoes bite him to see if that is how malaria spreads. The prestige of coming home a hero has superseded the soldier's normal tendency to value his good health.

Of course, the more radical the repositioning of the seven steps, the more difficult justifying the story's action becomes. Suppose, for example, we wrote a story in which step six was ranked above step two. Let us say that our story is about a man who loves reading so much he injures himself just so he can lie in a hospital bed for three months reading novels. Obviously, this is too radical a plot. Feasibility must be a byword when using the motivation scale.

With this examination of tension, we complete our look at ways to write both nonfiction and fiction. As a developing writer, you would be wise to try both forms of writing. Now that you have some specific writing patterns and systems to follow, you may discover that you have talent in both areas.

This shouldn't surprise you. After all, we began this section with a strong emphasis on the fact that good writing (of any kind) is nothing more than effective communication. If you keep that in mind, you won't go wrong.

In part 4 of this book, we will be analyzing ways in which you can take your finished manuscripts and get them into print. That is an important phase of the whole freelancing process. The world gains no benefit from your life-changing manuscripts if you keep them locked in your desk drawer. Don't keep your light under a bushel. So, read on and see how you can turn that candle into a spotlight.

PERSONALITY PROFILE FOR FICTIONAL CHARACTERS

Use this profile checklist to help yourself create and develop convincing characters in your fiction. A filled-in profile sheet can help you maintain consistent and believable characters in your writing.

1. Person's full legal name
2. Date of birth
3. Place of birth
4. Family information
   Father's occupation
   Mother's occupation
   Siblings' names and birth dates
   Famous or important relatives
   Family pets
   Father's and/or mother's philosophy of life/work
   Lessons learned from parents
5. Childhood history
   Friends and neighbors
   Childhood escapades, hobbies, accidents
6. Grade school name, location, and years attended
   Favorite teachers
   Favorite subjects
   Noteworthy incidents
7. High school name, location, and years attended
   Type of classes (vocational? college prep?)
   Sports participated in
   Scholastic honors
   Extracurricular activities
8. College names, locations, and years attended, if at all
   Degrees
   Majors and minors
   Scholarships, grants, honors, awards

9. Physical characteristics
   Height
   Weight
   Color of eyes
   Color of hair
   General health
   Gestures, mannerisms
   Tone of voice
   Facial expressions
   Manner of dress
   Size and appearance
   Demeanor
10. Office surroundings
   Desktop photos
   Wall hangings
   Room decor
11. Job title and responsibilities
   Part-time and/or summer jobs
   Career turning points
   Daily routine
   Philosophy of life/work
   Vocational goals
12. Personal triumphs and failures
13. Outstanding achievements
14. Pet peeves
15. Leisure activities
   Clubs, civic groups
   Avocations
   Reading preferences
   Arts enjoyed (music? dance? sculpture?)
   Sports and extracurricular activities
16. Future plans
17. Things the character wishes had been done differently at various stages

18. Military background
    Years of service and branch
    Highest held rank
    Medals, decorations, campaigns
19. Marriage and family
    Courtship
    Children, home life
20. World travel
21. Religious beliefs
22. Political leanings

PART IV

Marketing Strategies

Up to this point we have concentrated on ways in which you can learn to think, create, and work as a professional writer. Now it is time to discuss ways you can market your article and book manuscripts. But first, let's briefly review what we have learned so far.

We learned earlier that although competition in all areas of publishing is tough and standards of excellence are becoming more and more exacting, the field of publishing offers many opportunities for new writers to begin their careers.

The most successful approach to publishing is first to break into the small markets. Beginning writers should obtain as much training and experience as possible. The best way to do this is to give editors and readers material that will fascinate them, aiming for articles that have surefire never-miss topics. Having gained some experience, you are then prepared to follow advancement stages from small periodicals to national magazines to books.

So how do you start to gain that experience? How do you present your materials in a way that will catch an editor's eye? How do you increase the likelihood of your work being published? That's what we'll talk about here, and then we'll look at how to get the greatest financial return out of everything you write.

Some writers dislike talking about marketing their work. They believe that great writing should sell itself. But there's a name for people who don't "sell" their materials. They're called "unpublished writers."

If you want to be published, you have to sell your writing to the people who are "buying." You have to present your materials in such a manner that an editor will find that they fill a need. That's a lot easier to say than to do, so the next chapters give you specific ideas for marketing your work.

CHAPTER EIGHT

How to Sell Manuscripts

For many years I could not relate to people who said, "I just write for the fun of it." This was because I saw writing strictly as my occupation, never as a hobby or creative outlet. I considered myself a hired pen. Whatever needed to be written—article, short story, interview, book—I was ready and eager to produce it.

I admit that aspects of my writing career were often mundane or tedious, such as hours of researching in the library, typing out final drafts on the word processor, proofreading galleys, and racing against deadlines. The "fun" parts were seeing my byline in print, receiving royalty checks, and being the guest of honor at autograph parties.

However, as the years have passed, I have also discovered how to write for the enjoyment of it. Keeping journals has been therapeutic for me. Writing long letters by hand or e-mail has been a way to enhance friendships. Dabbling in poetry has sharpened my use of words. Creating jokes or short works of humor has proved to be entertaining. Indeed, writing can be *very* enjoyable. But even when done for pleasure, writing's impact on other people can only become a reality when that writing sees print. As such, we will now focus on specific procedures you can use to sell your manuscripts and book proposals.

DEFUSING REJECTIONS

The core strategy in all your marketing endeavors will be to provide editors and publishers with exactly the kind of manuscripts they are seeking. If you're not aware of what causes editors to reject material, that can work against you. So, let's look at the things of which you should be aware.

At writers' conferences I meet many writers who are armed with briefcases filled with rejected manuscripts. These people have poets' hearts, novelists' dreams, and dramatists' ill fate. They just can't understand why editors won't accept for publication what they write.

If you have ever found yourself wondering the same thing (and who hasn't?), maybe it's time to review your manuscripts. If your work gets rejection slips, perhaps it's because it falls into one of the following categories. Here are the twelve main things to beware of in order to limit rejections:

Avoid unprofessional appearance. Your manuscript should be on a good quality, white bond paper with one-inch margins and be set up in proper manuscript format. There should be no tears, smudges, or crossed-out lines anywhere. Use a laser or inkjet printer (not dot matrix) so that your work looks neat, distinct, and dark on the pages.

Avoid weak writing. Spelling, punctuation, grammar, and syntax should be perfect. The sentences should contain action verbs and visual nouns. Paragraphs should be short and blended together with good transitions. The manuscript should be written informatively and should be stylistically sound.

Avoid parody. The writing style should not be a copy of Stephen King, John Grisham, Joyce Carol Oates, Jan Karon, C. S. Lewis, or anyone else. It must be original to you: unique and distinctive.

Avoid second-rate topics. The subject of the manuscript should be something with wide appeal, something that is current in people's minds and is valuable to many readers. No matter how great a writing style is, an article about one's routine summer vacation will not interest most people.

Avoid technical terms. The manuscript should be written in nonprofessional language (no jargon, shoptalk, or trade lingo). It should use a variety of sentence lengths and be supplemented with examples, anecdotes, and perhaps some photos or charts. Readers should not be burdened with scientific mumbo-jumbo or technical chatter. As Joe Friday used to say on the old *Dragnet* show, "Just the facts, ma'am, just the facts!"

Avoid bias. Good writing does not present a prejudicial view of things. If articles are pro-Republican or pro-union or pro-Swedish or pro any other special-interest group, the feature will be of no use to editors of mass-marketed, general-interest publications. (Naturally, denominational or politically or ethnically based magazines are exceptions to this rule. They intend for you to be pro-Baptist, pro-Democrat, pro–Native American, or whatever they represent.)

Avoid poor timing. Feature stories need a news peg to make them timely. Seasonal material must be submitted four to six months in advance of holidays or seasonal changes. Christmas stories cannot be submitted to a magazine in late October or November. At that point they are not a month early, they are five months or more late.

Avoid an inappropriate tone. The "voice" of the manuscript must be in tune with the topic it is on. The writer should not give a light treatment to a serious matter, nor should a writer lecture when he or she is supposed to be teaching. Set the correct tone.

Avoid submitting materials to the wrong publisher. No matter how excellent a manuscript is, it will not be accepted unless it meets the needs of the publisher being contacted. For example, an excellent book on family finances might get rejected by a publishing house that specializes in religious-oriented books unless the book is filled with references to appropriate passages in the Bible. Likewise, don't send your novel or drama to a publisher that produces neither. Different publishers have different needs. Check out what publishers are producing your types of materials, or research your topic in the *Writer's Market* or *Christian Writers' Market Guide.* Likewise, avoid sending your query letter to an editor who left that publisher five years ago. Keep up-to-date on names by using the above volumes or address your letter generically ("The Editor").

Avoid shallow research. A book or article must support the claims it makes. Statements and pronouncements should be supported with references, quotations, and specific research.

Avoid outdated vocabulary. Slang, catch phrases, and clichés become quickly dated in the interim between when a manuscript is written, accepted, and finally published. As such, standard time-proven language should be relied upon when writing.

Avoid tediousness. Stories and articles that are solid narratives are flat, dull, and tedious. Readers want dialogue and quotations from other people. Most manuscripts are a fifty-fifty division between straight narration and quotations, as has been mentioned in two earlier chapters.

By avoiding the preceding pitfalls you will give a marketing edge to your manuscripts. You will also save yourself and several editors a lot of time and energy.

LITERARY AGENTS

Although writers of articles sell their own works, you may be wondering if marketing your book manuscript is something you will even want to bother with. Wouldn't it be better just to procure the services of a literary agent and let that person handle it? Well, that depends on what you expect from an agent.

An author's representative—or "literary agent" as he or she is more commonly called—is a person who represents a working writer. He or she sells the author's works, handles contract negotiations, arranges resales to paperback houses, and sometimes promotes sales to overseas outlets. Current lists of literary agents can be found in *Literary Market Place,* Sally Stuart's *Christian Writers' Market Guide,* and *Writer's Market,* all available at most bookstores or public libraries. Additional names and addresses may be obtained from the Writers Guild of America and the Society of Authors' Representatives.

Finding an agent is not as impossible as many beginning writers think it is. Your writing teachers, members of your writing club, or fellow working writers can sometimes help provide you with an introduction to an agent. Most of the large writers' conferences invite literary agents to take part in their week-long programs each year. Some agents even advertise their services in writers' magazines and publication trade papers.

Although the Society of Authors' Representatives (S.A.R.) has a passage in its bylaws which forbids members to advertise their services, many current S.A.R. members once did advertise in order to get a foothold in the business. Advertising is not necessarily a sign of a disreputable agent. Conversely, membership in a national organization is no foolproof guarantee of an agent's abilities or ethical conduct.

In choosing an agent, the things to look for are *reputation, rates,* and *recep-*

tion. The agent should have a reputation among your writing friends and colleagues as someone who is hard working and successful. The agent's rates should be no more than 15 percent on domestic sales and 20 percent on foreign sales. The agent's reception of your material should indicate an enthusiasm for your topic area and style of writing and an eagerness to work with you to make your manuscripts top publishing properties.

Personally, I have only used a literary agent on four occasions, whereas I have been able to sell dozens of book manuscripts and thousands of magazine articles on my own. One thing an agent can do that most writers cannot do is to hold an auction. If an agent feels you have a superb manuscript, he or she will send copies to eight or ten publishers who specialize in that kind of book. After giving the publishers time to read the book, the agent will set up a day on which to accept phone-call bids in an auction of the manuscript. When you consider hiring a literary agent, ask yourself these questions:

- Do I mind having a middleman between the publisher and me?
- Can I afford to pay 15 percent of my royalties to an agent?
- Am I seriously lacking in certain skills an agent could supplement for me, such as marketing, contract analysis, or publicity?
- If an agent handles my business matters, will that leave me more time to write?

If you decide to seek an agent, make the initial contact in writing. Submit a letter of introduction, a two-page autobiographical summary, some samples of your published material, and a proposal or synopsis of your latest work in progress. Enclose a stamped, self-addressed envelope. If the agent finds you and your work interesting, he or she will usually telephone you with requests for more samples of your writings. If those samples seem promising, an agreement of representation will be tendered for your consideration. With the signing of the agreement, the partnership will be legal.

Agents can be extremely helpful to authors. Just make sure the marriage of author and agent has a courting period of adequate time. Don't sign in haste and repent at leisure. In fact, if you aren't comfortable with the idea of having an agent help you with your writing and marketing, you might feel more at ease working with a coauthor. Sometimes that can be as effective as working with an agent.

COAUTHORS

As I have previously explained, I worked full time as a freelance writer for thirty years. Today, even as the full-time director of a university professional writing program, I still consider myself a full-time writer (especially during summer months when I'm not teaching). In any given month of the year, you can find me writing books (or articles or screenplays) on my own. Simultaneously, I also may be coauthoring a book with someone else. There are valid reasons why I never desert either camp.

My reasons for *not* working with a coauthor on some projects are mainly egotistical ones, I suppose. I sometimes like to reserve the byline for myself on certain projects if it will enhance my career. And I must admit, I enjoy keeping all the royalty payments for myself. See, I am human.

I also find it difficult to try to work with someone who either doesn't fully understand my views or whose experiences don't equal my own. Such situations lead to confusion, missed deadlines, and a poor final product. In those instances, I usually either offer to ghost the whole book for a flat fee or else I bow out of the project entirely. I advise you to consider those options as well if coauthoring doesn't work for you.

The Advantages
Still, there are many reasons why I *do* like coauthorship arrangements. Let me explain some of the advantages to you and in the process try to convince you of why such team efforts might benefit your writing.

Expanded sales potential. Even though coauthorship means you will have to split your royalty checks with someone else, you may end up earning just as much as you would have if you had written the book by yourself. How? Well, if you *and* your coauthor are both out busily appearing on radio and TV talk shows and at conferences and book fairs, you will have twice as many sales as you would have had if you were the sole author promoting the book. As a co-author your 5 percent of twenty thousand books sold is the same amount of money as 10 percent of ten thousand books sold. And, as sales volume increases, often so does the percentage rate authors receive. Once you've sold ten thousand copies, your royalty percentage may increase. So coauthorship is sometimes more profitable than solo writing.

Fame by association. If your coauthor is a well-known politician, business executive, minister, surgeon, or world explorer, you will share the limelight every time this famous person's new book is seen or talked about. It's your book, too. Thus, it's your fame, too. There's nothing wrong with shared popularity.

Different areas of expertise. Two specialists working together can create an outstanding book or article if each author will focus on his or her areas of expertise. For example, I once coauthored a national magazine feature, "Assertiveness Training for Your Child." My coauthor was Dr. L. Stanley Wenck, a child psychologist. He was an expert on raising and educating youngsters, and I was an expert on freelance writing and marketing. We combined our areas of specialization and produced a successful article for *Essence* magazine.

Different writing strengths. No two writers have identical writing strengths, and in coauthorship projects, that's good. That's particularly true when it comes to writing novels. Holly Miller, travel editor for the *Saturday Evening Post,* and I have coauthored some light romance novels under the pen name of Leslie Holden *(The Legacy of Lillian Parker, The Compton Connection,* and *The Caribbean Conspiracy).* Our styles complement each other. Holly has great abilities for developing characters: they have distinct ways of talking, dressing, and behaving, and each has an interesting personal history. On the other hand, I am more adept at creating tense action scenes, developing ironic plot twists, and writing terse, pensive dialogue. Holly provides the character depth, and I provide the plot pace. The end result is a balanced novel.

Overcoming procrastination. A writer working alone often works at a slow pace. This is often not the case with coauthors, however. With another author to encourage you, admonish you, and set deadlines for you, you find yourself driven to hold up your end of the workload. You work longer, harder, more creatively, and without the leisure of letting dangerous procrastination set in on you.

Problem solving. All writers occasionally write themselves into a corner and find themselves wondering how they will ever get their characters moving again. With a coauthor the solution is simple: You just send your chapter to your coauthor and attach a note saying, "What now?" A few days later you will get back one of two answers: "Start over" or "Try this idea." Either way, you're out of the corner.

The Logistics

There are a variety of ways to go about setting up a coauthorship work arrangement. Let me summarize some of the types I personally have been involved in and offer you a few opinions on each.

1. Team leader approach. This is usually used when a book is going to have one main author who will write more than 50 percent of the manuscript and a handful of contributing authors who will write the other half of the book (usually by receiving assignments to write one or two specific chapters on areas in their realm of expertise). These contributing authors are usually paid a flat fee (no royalty agreements) for their sections of the manuscript and are given "signature" bylines at the end of their chapters within the book, rather than a byline credit on the book's cover.

I was involved in a team leader project when Rita Berman was writing *The A–Z of Writing and Selling* (Moore Publishers). Rita wrote most of the book, but she contracted me to write a chapter on multiple marketing, Ruth Moose to write a chapter on selling fiction, Bette Elliott to write a chapter on writing syndicated columns, and Martha Monigle to write a chapter on ghostwriting. Only Rita's byline appeared on the cover, but we contributing authors were given signature bylines within the book and a publicity mention on the dust-jacket flyleaf.

Although I never received royalties from that book, I did receive a flat payment. That fact, combined with the publicity I received by being part of that coauthorship team, made it well worth the small amount of time and effort it took to write that one chapter.

2. Divided labors plan. This is the system I used when Stanley Field and I wrote a book on writing workshop techniques. This plan calls for two authors to devise a very specific outline for the nonfiction book they wish to write. They then dole out chapter assignments to each other and get to work.

The trick to making this system work is to have each coauthor serve as the other's editor. For example, in the book on writing workshops, when I finished my chapter on teaching journalism, I mailed it to Stanley. He read it, edited it, deleted any sections that overlapped something he had written for the book, and then sent the edited copy back to me to prepare in final draft form. When Stanley finished his chapter on teaching short stories, he sent it directly to me for a similar thorough editing. This kept our book organized, systematic, coordinated, and stylistically consistent.

The divided labors system will not work unless the coauthors maintain constant contact with each other. I know of one situation in which a publisher purposely teamed a brilliant psychologist with a popular author of children's books so that the twosome could produce a factually accurate but very readable book about how the human brain works. However, not grasping the publisher's logic in teaming them, the two authors took the book's outline and divided the chapters that needed to be written. The finished product was a disaster. The first chapter, by the psychologist, was so burdened with scientific terminology that only another psychologist could comprehend it. The second chapter, written by the children's book author, began, "The brain is our friend. It has two sides. One side is left. The other is right. The sides have different jobs." (I was subsequently hired to ghostwrite a whole new version of the manuscript and it was an overwhelming task.)

So, the key to the divided labors system is to work with a coauthor who is accessible, equal to you in writing and editing skills, and knowledgeable in specialty areas different from your own.

3. Ping-pong system. This is usually used in fiction writing by two authors who have a general idea of what their plot line is going to be, but not how they will bring it off. This is the technique Holly Miller and I use when writing our novels. I usually write the first two chapters and get the action rolling. Holly reads these chapters and then writes two chapters in which she "fleshes out" the characters I've created. Then, back and forth, we write one chapter each until the novel is finished. We only have general ideas of where the other author will next lead our characters, but this keeps the plot suspenseful even for us. Of course, we do discuss the book as it is progressing, and we edit each other's chapters along the way. Because we live far from each other, Holly and I use e-mail to discuss the works in progress and we attach the chapters to on-line messages we send to each other. We explain our developing images of the fictional characters, discuss our suggestions for possible future plot developments, and offer any ideas we have for new subplots. For us, it's a very workable system.

The drawback to the ping-pong system is that it's not easy to find a co-author who gels with your thinking and writing styles. Before teaming with Holly, I coauthored two *halves* of other novels with people I eventually had to admit I couldn't work with. Things either click or they don't. And the only way to find out if they can click is to give it a try.

Naturally, these three systems are not the only ways coauthorships can be arranged. I have been involved in many other varieties. For example, I once submitted an article to *Essence* called "How to Overcome Shyness." About the same time, Wista Johnson submitted a similar article there. The editors liked both articles, so they bought both and then culled sections from each to form a new article that carried both of our bylines. So, Wista and I became coauthors, and to this day we have never met or communicated with each other. (I later took my original version, modified it to fit the Christian market, and sold it to Regular Baptist Press as "How and Why Christians Should Overcome Shyness.")

Truly, there are an infinite number of ways you can become a coauthor. If you have never tried any of them, let me suggest that you give one a chance. My guess is, you will discover the whole bonus realm of creativity and marketing that teamwork efforts can give you.

If two heads are better than one, just imagine what two hearts, two ambitions, and two pens can do. The sky's the limit!

GHOSTWRITING

A moment ago I mentioned the term *ghostwriting*. Since ghostwriting is another writing skill you can market, perhaps we should take the time now to discuss how it's done.

Authors will tell you they write to inspire people or to share knowledge or to entertain readers or to chronicle events. That may be true. However, unless authors also write to earn money, they won't write *anything* for long because computers, supplies, and stamps are expensive. That's where ghostwriting comes in. There is an ethical argument that can be made against ghostwriting. Some people think that putting one person's name on a book written by someone else is both theft of one person's work and the propagation of a lie. To some extent, I can understand those views.

So then, why do I work as a ghostwriter? The only two answers I can give you are these: (1) most readers are not naive enough to believe that all those sports and entertainment and political personalities with best-selling auto-biographies really wrote those books about themselves; and (2) I would rather have a well-written book released by a ghostwriter than a lousy book written by the bylined author. Publishers who charge from $15 to $50 for a book need to make sure that the buyer is getting a quality product while providing the ideas and concepts of the person whose name appears on the book as "author." Thus, ghosting meets both of those needs by having the named person tell his or her story and life lessons to someone who can write them in a readable and capti-vating way. However, because of the desire to not "deceive" the public, many publishers (especially Christian ones) use a "with" byline for the writer rather than keeping the writer a mystery. That's why so many autobiographies come out with an author line that reads "Famous Person with Hardworking Writer."

Books are expensive, and people deserve to get a quality product for their money. It might shock you to discover how many "ghosts" are doing the actual writing of syndicated columns that carry the byline of a famous doctor or chef or retired politician. If you have ever wondered how popular TV evangelists can find the time to write one or two new books each year, the answer is, they can't. They often hire people to assist them with research, writing, editing, and typing.

If you are considering the idea of ghosting, let me give you some perspec-tives on it. As a ghost, you will get no byline credits for anything you write, and you will not even be able to use a tear sheet from one of your ghostwritten articles or books as a reference to show a new editor or publisher (although you can certainly tell this to an editor orally). Your payment will be either a flat fee or as low as a 2 percent royalty; the rest of the royalties will go to the bylined author. You will not be invited on publisher-sponsored promotional tours for the book. In effect, you will be invisible—a true ghost.

There is a bright side, however. While researching the book, you will be able to travel on an expense account if the publisher agrees to this in advance. Usually, all of the advance money will go directly to you (from $6,000 to $45,000 or more depending on the project). Expenses are reimbursed to you separately. Your name will usually appear on the acknowledgments page of the book.

In short, if you want to write for money first and prestige second, ghost-writing is for you. Now, let's see how it's done. Suppose you are approached by someone who wants you to write a 250-page manuscript. The two of you will usually meet for a free initial consultation to discuss the type of book needed, the deadline for the project, and the focus and purpose for the book.

Based on this discussion, you must determine how many work hours of research and writing it will take for you to write the book *and* how much it will cost to have the rough and final draft manuscripts typed and photocopied.

Using the book ghosting estimate worksheet (see end of chapter), you can outline for your client exactly what costs will be involved. Most writers charge a flat fee for writing time and a half-price rate for research and editing. Under "Writing First Complete Draft," you might note *100 hours* at a per-hour rate of *$20* for a cash fee total of *$2,000.* Under "Editing Second Draft," however, you may note only *4 hours* at *$10* per hour for a cash fee of *$40.* Any fees incurred for original research would be in addition to all this.

Your "Typing" and "Miscellaneous Expenses" will have to be estimated after you have contacted a typist (who can transcribe tapes, too) and you have checked on prices of needed materials. Remember to include estimates of all costs, both for your time and your out-of-pocket expenses.

If the client accepts your bid, draw up a statement of agreement as to what both parties expect from the arrangement. Both parties should sign it and then have it witnessed and dated. Ask for half your advance money upon the closing of the contract and half upon the completion of the manuscript.

As you work on the book, keep a time record (see end of chapter) of how you spend your day. Under "Clock Hours" you might note that you worked on the book from 9:00 to 11:30 A.M. at a "Billing Total" of *$50* and that you completed the preface to the book. If the client should ever come by to ask, "How's it going?" you will be able to document your progress. If you are given money from the book advance, that will be credited against the total final billing for the project.

To advertise your ghostwriting services, you can put an ad in the trade publications (*Writer's Journal, The Writer,* and *The Christian Communicator,* for example) and send notices to writers' clubs (and their club newsletters), or send your résumé to various publishers with a cover letter announcing your availability as a ghostwriter. If you follow these procedures, there is not a ghost of a chance you won't succeed!

QUERY LETTERS AND PROPOSALS

Whether you are working with a literary agent or plan to market your articles and books independently, you will need to know how to write effective query letters and book proposals.

Quality presentation of important information is key for freelancers. All freelance writers need business cards or letterhead with their name, address, e-mail address, and phone and/or fax number printed on them. These can be printed in bulk or reproduced one at a time on your home computer and word-processing software.

Contacting editors with query letters helps to line up regular assignments. Send query letters to specific editors, using their names rather than just their job titles when you write to them. Write your letters in a lively, captivating manner, yet be very specific in providing such details about your article as length, date available, topic, accompanying photos, and your credentials for writing the piece.

Query letters for articles and books differ in their details, so we will deal with them one at a time, starting with article queries.

Querying Periodicals
Before approaching any magazine you need to know *how* to approach them. Each magazine is different: some want query letters, some want proposals, some want completed manuscripts. To save time in preparing queries and manuscripts according to each magazine's particular dictates, obtain a copy

of the magazine's guidelines for writers. These guidelines will outline the magazine's payment rate, publication schedule, photographic needs, readership profiles, areas of interest, and editorial personnel. You need the managing editor's name so that you can send your query letter addressed to that person. These guidelines can be found on the publication's Web site or you can send a self-addressed, stamped envelope (SASE) to the magazine and request a copy.

A query letter is a one-page, single-spaced letter sent to a magazine editor outlining an idea for a potential article. It is wise not to write your article first and then try to sell it. However, if the editor does not know your work, a completed manuscript may be required at first. The editor may like your idea but may want a slightly different slant or perhaps 250 fewer words than you had wanted to use. Get your authorization and specific instructions, *then* write the article (unless the editor insists on a completed article before considering the idea). Check a publication's writer's guidelines to see its policy on this. Only about 20 percent of magazines insist on seeing completed pieces.

For magazines that say they do not read unsolicited manuscripts, a query letter is mandatory in order to get clearance to submit your manuscript. In writing your query letter be as specific as possible in your explanations of what your article will be about. Do not ask an editor if she would like to see an article on traveling in Europe since that is too general and too ambiguous; instead, ask if she would be interested in an article on "Skydiving into the Canals of Venice" (the article I mentioned earlier in the book). Be point-blank in pinning down your article ideas.

Always make sure that your article idea is appropriate for the magazine you are contacting. Just as a review of the annual conference of the Southern Baptist Convention will not be accepted by the editor of *Today's Lutheran Woman,* neither will a feature on nine ways to make spicy pumpkin pie be accepted by the editor of *Weight Watchers Magazine.* Whether selling to religious or secular periodicals, you must give the editors what they need.

Be unique in what you offer. Study back issues of the magazine you are contacting so that you will not be offering a topic the magazine has covered recently. Don't be dull. Make your letter interesting, captivating, intriguing. Your query letter is a sales piece. How competent are you at selling ideas? You will need to be good. This business is competitive.

Make sure that your grammar is correct, your spelling is perfect (this includes using end-of-line hyphenations correctly), and your typing is clean. Suggest to the editor how long you feel the article can be, how many photos or other graphics you can send with it (cartoons, maps, etc.), and how soon you can have it ready to send.

Mention only autobiographical material that may apply to the article being discussed in the letter. For example, if your article topic were "Pros and Cons of Corporal Punishment," it would be appropriate to note that you are a sixth-grade teacher and also the mother of two elementary-age schoolchildren. But if you are a florist, why bother mentioning it since it has no bearing on your perspective of the subject at hand?

In closing, briefly thank the editor for his or her time and then sign off. Make sure that your return address, phone number, e-mail address, and fax number (if you have one) are at the top of the page. Remember to include a stamped, self-addressed envelope. If you receive no reply in three weeks, send a follow-up postcard or e-mail asking about the status of your query letter. If you receive no replies to anything within five weeks, feel free to try elsewhere.

As you write more and more query letters, the process will become more natural for you. Once it does, you'll be ready to step up to a greater challenge: the book proposal.

Writing Book Proposals

Selling book ideas requires preparation of a more involved query known as a book proposal. Forget the scary rumors you have heard. Here is the fact: Book proposals *do* get read by publishers. What's more, many unknown writers *do* get contracts thanks to well-written proposals.

Before you even write the proposal, you need to be sure of two elements.

First, you will need a fascinating subject—a very commercial topic. Publishers need to make money from their books. Quite often the choice of subject alone can be the selling factor for a book; so, choose carefully. It's easy to find ideas for books. One way is to read *Books in Print, Forthcoming Books, 80 Years of Best Sellers,* or *Subject Guide to Books in Print* (all published by R. R. Bowker) in the reference section of your library. Discover topics that have never been covered or have not been covered adequately. Also read contemporary periodicals, look for a fascinating article on a unique subject, and then do enough research on the topic to write a whole book about it.

Your second need is to be convinced *yourself* that your book idea is a good one and that it should be given the go-ahead as a writing project. To determine the merit of the book's concept, test it with these questions:

- Am I truly qualified to write this book?
- Am I really excited about doing this book?
- Have I prepared myself to write a book?
- Does this topic have broad universal appeal?
- Of what value will this book be to readers?
- What audience will I aim for? Adults? Children? Laypeople? Professionals? Senior citizens?
- Will my material become outdated quickly?
- Have too many books already been written on this subject?

If after answering these questions you still have faith in your book idea, your next move will be to find a potential publisher. Study Jeff Herman's *Insider's Guide to Editors, Publishers and Literary Agents* (Prima Publishing), *Writer's Market* (Writer's Digest Books), *Writer's Handbook* (The Writer, Inc.), and Sally Stuart's *Christian Writer's Market Guide* (Harold Shaw Publishers) to locate those who publish the kind of book you intend to write. Many publishers specialize in self-help books or children's literature or some other topic. If your book falls into a specific category, concentrate first on contacting the publishers who emphasize that category in their catalogs. Eliminate from your list any publishing houses that don't accept unsolicited manuscripts or who deal only with literary agents. Unless the publisher is willing to read unsolicited submissions, your time and postage will be wasted. (Note that there are manuscript services in the Christian publishing world, such as The Writer's Edge and the service offered by the Christian Bookseller's Association that allow you, for a fee, to reach publishers that do not accept unsolicited manuscripts. See the *Christian Writers' Market Guide* for more information.)

Many novice writers wonder if proposal submissions should be sent to ten or twelve publishers simultaneously. Most publishers do not prefer this, so I usually recommend contacting only one at a time, but then not allowing any more than six weeks to pass without a response. If you do elect to send out multiple submissions (as is common practice among literary agents), make sure that you indicate in your cover letter that your proposal is being sent to other publishers.

The cover letter itself should be a real carnival barker's pitch. It must really *sell* your book idea. Don't be coy or reserved. Be excited, specific, optimistic, and purposeful. Stress the fact that yours is a different idea and that even when dealing with older ideas you have new facts, statistics, examples, sources, views, experiences, and approaches. Here are the things to focus on in your cover letter:

- The estimated length in pages or words the book will be when finished
- The amount of time you will need to complete the book
- Your credentials for writing the book (including academic preparation, job-related experience, personal interest in the topic, and previous writing credits)
- Your projected markets for the book (Colleges? Bookstores? Book clubs? Libraries? Lecture tours?) and any special-interest or buying groups willing to use or promote this book?
- Your ability to promote the book on radio, TV, at readings, as well as through your church or other avenues of publicity

Once you've written your cover letter, you need to prepare a synopsis. It should have the excitement of a dustjacket blurb along with the detail of a *New Yorker* book review. Explain what the book will cover, how it will cover it, what format will be used, and what unique things will appear in the text. The synopsis is separate from the cover letter and should be limited to one page (about 275 words).

Next, prepare a table of contents along with another, more detailed, summary or outline. The outline should list the title of the book and the title of each chapter. Under each chapter title it should offer a one-paragraph summary of what is to be covered in that chapter. Choose book and chapter titles that are provocative or humorous or controversial or filled with human drama. If a title arrests the editor's attention, half your sales battle is won. (One of the units in my book *Staying Ahead of Time* was about how to make use of layover time at an airport. I called that unit, "Overcoming Terminal Problems." The acquisitions editor responded to the intriguing title in my proposal and asked for more.)

Your one-paragraph summaries should be succinct overviews of what the chapters will cover. They should mention, too, if the chapters will contain certain sidebars, reading lists, graphs, charts, illustrations, maps, or photographs. Generally, chapters should be designed to be about fifteen to twenty-five type-written pages long.

When submitting your proposal, you will need to send two completed chapters or one chapter and an introduction. The completed package must also include a stamped, self-addressed envelope so that the publisher can respond at your expense, at least initially. If the publisher is willing to look at your proposal via e-mail, all the better, but ask before sending it. (Most editors will refuse to open an attachment from a writer unknown to him or her.)

By way of review, here are the items needed for a book proposal:

- a cover letter
- a basic table of contents
- a nine-hundred- to one-thousand-word synopsis
- a detailed table of contents
- two sample chapters
- a stamped, self-addressed envelope

If an editor becomes interested in your book idea, he or she will respond to your proposal in one of three ways: (1) by offering a contract; (2) by asking to see more sample chapters before making a decision; or (3) by countering with another idea, such as teaming you with a coauthor for the book or changing the book's focus in order to reach a different audience.

But no matter which of the three responses you receive, they all lead to the same end—a published book carrying your byline.

PREPARING THE MANUSCRIPT

Once the query or book proposal has received the editor's approval, meaning a publishing house has contracted the book or an editor has assigned you the article idea, and the material has been written, your work will need to be sent in a standard manuscript format (see the sample title page at the end of this chapter).

Put your legal name, Social Security number, and address on four single-spaced lines in the upper left corner of the first page. In the upper right corner indicate the rights you are offering, a notice as to whether the piece is fiction or nonfiction, and a word count to the nearest twenty-five words. Since most word-processing programs include a word count feature, many editors expect an exact word count. To do that, make certain you only "grab" the word count for your content, leaving the words of your byline and address information or other added details out of that total figure. (See the "Standard Manuscript Lengths" section at the end of this chapter to look up word-count estimates for various types of manuscripts.)

After you've put in word count, center your title about a third of the page from the top. Capitalize only the first letters of the key words in the title. Double-space and then center your byline. If you use a pen name, it goes under the title, but your real name still must go in the upper left corner of the page before your copyright information.

Leave one-inch margins on all sides. Double-space every line in your manuscript, including block quotations and footnotes. If the manuscript is an article, at the bottom of each page type the word *more* in parentheses if it continues to another page. When the article is finished, type "End" centered under the last line. For books and articles, at the top of page two and all succeeding pages, type your last name, a key word from the title, and the page number.

When typing the body of the text, underline or italicize all foreign words that are uncommon. Taco and résumé are common American usage, so they do not need to be underlined; however, a Latin phrase such as *cum grano salis* ("with a grain of salt") should be italicized or underlined. If your computer keyboard or word-processing program is not equipped with accent marks or diacritical marks and you need to put those in separately, use a dark ink pen. Always keep copies of your manuscripts on your hard drive and a separate disk, stored in a secure location. Book publishers usually want a hard copy of the manuscript as well as an electronic version. For magazines you can often just submit the electronic version, usually by e-mail.

When mailing the manuscript of an article, put a piece of thin cardboard in a nine-by-twelve-inch manila envelope and send the pages of the manuscript unfolded. If photos are enclosed, they should be pressed between pieces of cardboard that are taped together.

Book manuscripts should be mailed in a box, such as a typing-paper or photographic-paper box. The pages should be numbered throughout and put into the box loose, without staples or paper clips.

Manuscripts sent by "snail" mail should be sent by first-class or priority mail. (A new postal feature allows you to purchase for a small fee a tracking code by which you can trace items sent by priority mail.) Follow up with the editor to be sure the package arrived.

To keep track of your manuscript, maintain a manuscript submission record (see section at the end of this chapter) for each of your circulating articles or short stories or books. Review these sheets at the beginning of each week and send follow-up cards on any delinquent reports.

If you are wondering what may be the easiest way to get a toe in the publishing waters so that you can gain experience in writing and submitting manuscripts, I suggest that you consider becoming a regional correspondent for a national magazine or perhaps for one of your state's large newspapers. We will look at that in the next chapter.

WORKSHEET: BOOK GHOSTING ESTIMATE

Project: _____

Author: _____ **Publisher:** _____

Estimated Per-Hour Fees

	Hours	Rate Per Hour	Total Fee
Preliminary Work			
Consultations	_____	_____	_____
Basic concept writing	_____	_____	_____
Queries to publishers	_____	_____	_____
Research	_____	_____	_____
Structuring	_____	_____	_____
Synopsis preparation	_____	_____	_____
Outline	_____	_____	_____
Writing	_____	_____	_____
Three sample chapters	_____	_____	_____
First complete draft	_____	_____	_____
Editing	_____	_____	_____
For second draft	_____	_____	_____
For final draft	_____	_____	_____
Typing	_____	_____	_____
Preliminary	_____	_____	_____
Final draft	_____	_____	_____
Administration	_____		_____
Total Fees for Writing			_____

Expenses	_____
Miscellaneous	_____
Tape transcripts	_____
Photocopying	_____
Telephone	_____
Outside consultants	_____
Postage	_____
Research	_____
Travel	_____
Lodging	_____
Meals	_____
Supplies	_____
Photos	_____
Miscellaneous fees	_____
TOTAL	_____

Make sure your projected total expenses are significantly less than the fees you'll be able to bill. If not, this is a losing proposition. Take it only if you feel it's worth the experience.

TIME RECORD

Date Received: _____ **Deadline:** _____

Project: _____

Date	Clock Hours	Billing Total	Remarks/Accomplishments

Below is a sample title page for articles. For a book you would not list anything about what rights are offered and you would not type "more" at the bottom of the pages.

Legal Name*	**Copyright © Year, Name**
Social Security Number	**Rights Offered**
Address	**Fiction/Nonfiction**
City, State, Zip Code	**Word Count Here**

Article or Story Title Goes Here
By Your Name (Legal or Pen Name)*

The body of the article or short story goes here. These lines should all be typed double-spaced. Remember to use a dark ribbon, clean typing keys, and a good quality bond grade of paper. Always do a careful job of proofreading before you submit your manuscript.

(more)

* *If a work is written under a pseudonym, the author may wish to write his or her legal name and then place the pseudonym or byline name in the upper left portion of the page, in the following manner:*

Dennis E. Hensley
(Leslie Holden)
Address

Manuscript Type	Average Word Count
Children's picture books:	500 to 1,000 words
Juvenile books:	20,000 to 80,000 words
Movie scripts:	90 to 120 pages *(Scripts are calculated on the formula that one page, with stage directions and character dialogue typed on separate lines, equals one minute of screen time.)*
Nonfiction books:	15,000 to 200,000 words
Novellas:	5,000 to 16,000 words
Hard cover novels:	25,000 to 150,000 words
Original paperback novels:	35,000 to 80,000 words
Poems:	4 to 16 lines
Short-short stories:	800 to 2,500 words
Short stories:	2,600 to 4,000 words
Speeches:	2,800 words *(equals a half-hour when read aloud; about 100 words per minute of speech time)*
TV scripts	20 to 30 pages *(equals one half-hour show; see note under "Movie Scripts")*
Curtain-raiser plays:	20 to 30 pages
Three-act plays:	90 to 120 pages

Manuscript Submission Record

Title of Manuscript: _____

Word Count: _____

___Book Proposal

___Fiction ___Nonfiction ___Interview ___Profile

___Poetry ___Special Project: _____

Photos Mailed with MS: _____

Agent: _____ Coauthor: _____

___Used Real Byline ___Pen Name of _____

Date Mailed: _____   Date Mailed: _____

Sent To: _____   Sent To: _____

Purchase Price: _____   Purchase Price: _____

Date Rejected: _____   Date Rejected: _____

Editor's Remarks: _____   Editor's Remarks: _____

_____   _____

_____   _____

_____   _____

Date Mailed: _____   Date Mailed: _____

Sent To: _____   Sent To: _____

Purchase Price: _____   Purchase Price: _____

Date Rejected: _____   Date Rejected: _____

Editor's Remarks: _____   Editor's Remarks: _____

_____   _____

_____   _____

_____   _____

CHAPTER NINE

Maximum Return, Minimum Effort

Effective marketing of a writer's time and talent begins with the understanding that writing is, at best, difficult work; as such, it should earn for the writer a good return on the hour. But a good return is not always the case, unless the writer knows how best to channel his or her efforts to ensure that even minimum efforts can lead to maximum income earnings.

The purpose of this final chapter will be to pass along to you some of the "street savvy" that will help you advance your writing career quickly, save you a great deal of time and energy, and substantially increase your annual income derived from freelance writing. Let's begin by discovering one of the easiest ways to guarantee regular cash flow and steady bylines.

REGIONAL CORRESPONDENCE

One of the best ways for a beginning freelance writer to gain experience, obtain regular bylines, and earn some money is to become a regional correspondent for a newspaper, magazine, or denominational publication.

The regional correspondent, or "stringer," covers news that occurs in a specific area—one city, one county, or perhaps one state—and reports that news on a regular basis to the home office of the publication he or she writes for. For example, during the four years in which I lived in the small town of North Manchester, Indiana, I worked as a regional correspondent for the *Fort Wayne News-Sentinel.* If anything newsworthy occurred in my town or county, I would look into it and either phone or mail in a story about it to the Fort Wayne newspaper, forty-five miles away.

Since it is virtually impossible for major statewide newspapers to cover all newsworthy events in each of the towns in which they are circulated, the newspapers are eager to find qualified correspondents to assist in this process. The correspondents usually file brief reports on local election results, new local laws, school board meetings, major automobile accidents, intriguing local crimes, important business developments, and such annual events as festivals, parades, high-school seasonal play-offs, and church socials. Additionally, correspondents occasionally contribute journalistic profiles of local civic, business, and religious leaders.

Denominational magazines need regional writers as well, writers who report on statewide church conventions, church groundbreakings and renovations, new pastoral assignments, and various radio, auditorium, or TV ministries.

To become a regional correspondent, write a letter (see sample letter at the end of this chapter) to the managing editor of a periodical that is available in your town, yet has a base some distance away. In the letter explain that you wish to become a regional correspondent for that publication. Mention your credentials and experience. You may wish to include a sample article of current news value. If you have written for other publications, send along copies of two or three of your printed articles.

Once accepted as a correspondent, you will be given a press card that will give you access to meetings and social events at which members of the press corps are given privileged treatment. Although you will carry a press card, technically you still will be a freelance writer. The newspaper or magazine will not put you on salary; you will be paid according to the number of articles and news items you turn in. You will not be given any of the benefits that full-time staff reporters receive (retirement benefits, worker's compensation insurance, paid vacations, or dental coverage); however, you also will not have to work the set hours of a full-time reporter.

The best benefit you will receive as a regional correspondent will be the opportunity you will have to cover a story for a periodical but not have to sell all rights to your story to that periodical. This enables you to resell your articles later to other publications. And that's a real benefit. Let me explain.

A full-time reporter who works for a newspaper or magazine as a salaried employee is said to be doing work-for-hire. This means the employer *owns* all rights to the articles the reporter writes for the periodical. You, however, are not on salary. Once your freelance article appears in the periodical you work for as a regional correspondent, you then can market your article elsewhere.

Here's an example of how it works. Let's say that a famous evangelist has been asked to come to your city to help celebrate the opening of a new church. While in town, this person grants you an interview. Naturally, you will quickly write or call in your interview to the periodical you are working for as a regional correspondent. Soon, your article will be printed in that publication. After that, you are free to reclaim possession of your article (as well as your notes, your taped interview, and your photographs of the evangelist) and begin to market the same article, or variations of it, to other magazines and newspapers. In this way, you may wind up making six or eight article sales, whereas the salaried reporter is limited to just one sale to his or her employer's publication.

As you can quickly figure out, being a regional correspondent will not only keep you busy for one periodical, it will also provide many opportunities for you to do spin-off marketing of your articles and features. It is an excellent way for the beginning freelance writer to get involved in the publishing process.

MULTIPLE MARKETING

As I mentioned, one of the great advantages of being a regional correspondent or general freelance writer is the option you have to sell your article several times. Multiple marketing is a practice I have used for many years.

I learned that I could train my ears and eyes to detect article ideas everywhere I went. What's more, by applying a few professional modifications, I found I could resell an original news item to several statewide newspapers and national magazines. You can do the same thing by following a few basic steps.

When selling one article idea to several publications, I use an approach geared to ever-enlarging markets. I sell first to the city paper, then to large statewide papers, then to regional periodicals, then to the national outlets and, whenever possible, to international publications. Each time I resell the article idea, I try to make the new version different in at least three ways.

- *Photos.* I provide photos of the person or event that have not appeared in other publications.
- *Facts.* I insert one or two new facts about the incident that were not emphasized in a previous article.
- *Format.* I attempt to write the article as stylistically close to the established format of the receiving publication as possible, while also trying to slant the piece to the publication's geographic locale.

Here's an example: A man in my area named Peter Schlatter invented a workable two-wheel automobile, and I played the story for all it was worth. My first article appeared in the *Muncie Star,* a city paper, with a local-boy-makes-good angle. It mentioned area people who had influenced Schlatter, and it gave a short history of his years in town. My next article appeared in the *Muncie Weekly News,* a countywide paper, with an area-resident-is-inventor angle. I next sold the article to the magazine sections of the *Indianapolis Star* and the *South Bend Tribune,* two statewide papers, with a Hoosier-man-is-unique-mechanic angle. The article covered statewide auto shows at which the car had been displayed. Afterward, I sold the article to *Collision,* a national publication, focusing strictly on the auto itself, and it eventually went international when I sold it to United Press International for its overseas and Canadian editions. Milking an article is a trick of the trade for a small-town writer who enjoys a worldwide audience.

A lot of the drudgery of freelance writing can be eliminated when the writer sells an article a second and third time. Checks and bylines are still the end products, but the research and interviewing and most of the original draft writing are no longer necessary. You simply retain all rights to your articles by putting the natural copyright symbol on your manuscripts in the upper right corner of the first page (e.g., Copyright © 2004 by Dennis E. Hensley) and then assume ownership after each subsequent publication of your article. Some publications will say in their guidelines that they want to buy exclusive or "all rights" to freelance submissions. It is best either to avoid these publications or to negotiate in advance your copyright ownership of your material. Let me say again as I did in chapter 2 that some freelance writers do not like to put the copyright symbol on the manuscript since under the new copyright laws the material is protected anyway. I, however, am a fanatic about wanting to establish the date at which I wrote and sold each article so that I can later verify my ownership should any question of plagiarism ever arise.

My marketing rule of thumb is that I seldom write an article unless I am confident that I can market it (or a modified version of it) to at least four or more publications. This is where writing about the topics you love is important, so that you won't tire of the subject on which you are focusing so frequently. Even seemingly minor news ideas can be sold to a variety of markets if you get the right news peg.

To follow the step-by-step reselling technique more closely, let's look at the time I marketed an interview conducted with Charlotte and Walter Baldwin, the mother- and father-in-law of the Reverend Jim Jones of the Guyana mass suicides, which took place in November of 1978. By retracing my steps, we will see how the multiple marketing process works.

When I visited the Baldwins in their home, I went prepared with dozens of questions. I recorded a long interview that touched on a number of topics, including their daughter's marriage to and life with Jim Jones. I also asked the Baldwins to provide me with photos of their daughter, Marceline, and Jim Jones taken at their wedding and at family reunions. Additionally, I made photographs of the local school and church that Marceline and Jim had attended. I also took my own photos of the Baldwins.

After the interview, I processed my photos and wrote my feature based on the interview. I kept the first draft short—about one thousand words. I took the draft to the editor of my local paper, the *North Manchester News Journal,* and asked if he would like to buy it. He said yes but explained to me that his budget for freelance material was limited. I let him print the article and two photos in exchange for $45, a byline, and two dozen free copies of the edition in which it appeared. It was agreed that ownership of the article would be mine.

Once that local article appeared in print, I sent a copy of it to the editor of the weekend magazine supplement for the *South Bend Tribune.* I asked if I could expand the article to two thousand words, add some extra pictures, and sell it to him. His paper covered most of northern Indiana and southern Michigan, and he realized that very few of his readers would have seen the version I did for the North Manchester paper. He offered me a byline and $250 and four free copies of the printed version. I agreed, but again retained ownership.

After the article broke in South Bend, I sent a copy of it to the editor of the *Cincinnati Enquirer* (both a typed manuscript copy and a photocopy of the in-print version). He knew that none of his readers would have seen the Indiana newspapers; so, he paid me $400 and gave me a byline and five free printed copies for one-time rights to reprint the *South Bend Tribune* article exactly as I had written it.

I continued this same process of sending my article to different editors of different papers in different states. I never hid the fact that the article had already appeared in other newspapers. The editors never seemed to mind, so long as the other newspapers did not cross over into their circulation or reader-ship territories.

While my general feature on the Baldwins was making the rounds of editors in Indiana, then Ohio, then Kentucky, then Michigan, and so on, and was earning payment checks for me on a steady basis, I went on to a new project. I replayed my interview tapes and pulled out information I had not already covered. I produced a second manuscript focusing strictly on Mrs. Baldwin's relationship with her daughter after Marceline's marriage to Reverend Jones. I then started it on the same circuit of editors.

You can do the same sort of thing with your articles. You just need to remember a few basic points related to multiple article sales.

First, remember to do a long interview or a lot of other research so that you will have plenty of topics to write about.

Second, maintain copyright ownership of your articles and manuscripts.

Third, sell to the smallest markets first and then to larger and larger circulation publications.

Fourth, focus on researching articles that will have enough broad appeal to sell to several different periodicals.

Resales can increase a freelance writer's income by more than 60 percent in one year's time when used effectively. And since one of the reasons for writing is to be paid for your work, doesn't that make a lot of sense?

WRITING ARTICLES AND BOOKS
SIMULTANEOUSLY

We have now seen that there are a variety of ways to write a manuscript (co-authorship, ghostwriting, regional corresponding) and to market it (query letters, book proposals, multiple marketing plans). You now are ready to see how article writing, book writing, and multiple marketing can be done simultaneously, and, thus, can triple your work output and your earnings.

Of the two most difficult challenges a freelancer faces, I believe marketing is far tougher than writing. For that reason, I have developed a successful marketing system that both lines up a string of advance sales and predetermines the kind of writing needed for those sales. The system is three-phased:

- Phase One: Develop and write a series of articles on a specific topic for a specific magazine.
- Phase Two: Combine the series articles and sell them as a book.
- Phase Three: Sell excerpts from the published book.

I have written several books and many began as a series of articles in one or more magazines. Let me take you step by step through the process I used in marketing my book *Staying Ahead of Time* (Bobbs-Merrill Publishing).

Step 1: Look for a Multifaceted Topic

First find a topic of interest to yourself and other readers. Make the topic diverse enough to be analyzed from many perspectives. In my case, I chose the topic of time management.

Step 2: Prepare an Extensive Outline of Your Book

Decide what the structure of your nonfiction book will be. You will need chapters on the background of your subject, its case histories, past and current research on the topic, reviews of current literature written about it, interviews with experts in the field, and commentaries on innovations, new concepts, and experiments related to this topic.

For my time management book I decided to have a unit on how people throughout the ages have measured, valued, and used time (background, case histories). I also decided to interview numerous successful business and civic leaders to learn about the systems they used for managing time (interviews, commentaries, experiments, innovations). Finally, I determined to try to develop some new systems of my own (new concepts) and to prepare a suggested reading list (current literature) for the book's appendix.

Step 3: Focus on Specific Problems

From your large overview of the topic, splinter off one particular problem. In an article, discuss and solve the problem. Once you've developed the basic outline for the book, build the book article by article, selling each one as it is written. This will help the reader keep each marketing phase going.

One small but nagging problem people told me they had in managing time was in knowing what to do with themselves during a long layover at an airport terminal. I prepared the article I mentioned to you earlier called "Overcoming Terminal Problems," which described ten useful activities a person could do during a layover.

I sold the airport article as a freelance piece to *Roto* magazine in Indiana and then to *Gulfshore Life* in Florida. I sent tear sheets of both published articles to the editor of *Market Builder* magazine (a publication geared toward people in sales) and suggested a one-year, twelve-article series on time management.

The editor was impressed with the idea. She said yes. She bought from me the reprint rights to the airport article as the first feature for the series. Bingo! I now had eleven future article sales guaranteed.

I continued to move through my book outline, finding more and more time management problems to solve or systems to report on. Each became a new feature article. I sent each original article to the editor of *Market Builder* and kept the originals on my hard drive for my records (with backup copies on disk).

My agreement with *Market Builder* had three points: Each article was to be paid for upon acceptance; copyright ownership would rest with me, as author; and, once each new article appeared in *Market Builder*, I was free to sell it anywhere else I chose.

I finished all twelve articles for the series in nine weeks and received full payment for them. During the next year as each article appeared in *Market Builder*, I began to resell that feature to other markets. (This provided bonus cash, plus additional byline exposure.) A few modifications of the *Market Builder* features would redirect the articles to vacationers, senior citizens, students, or whatever new markets I might be focusing on.

Step 4: Prepare Folders on the Topics
As you do research on the topics covered in your projected chapters, keep all of your scribbled notes, published features, and rough drafts of new articles in folders labeled by each chapter title. This is in addition to the transcribed interview notes and final draft manuscripts on that topic you've kept in electronic form.

Step 5: Write the Book's Chapters
With advance money in your pocket from the sale of your series, as well as regular reprint sales being made each month, you can take time out to write your book. Take all of the material in one of your chapter folders and form it into a chapter. Take your published articles on that chapter's general topic and link them together with subtitles, transitional anecdotes, and filler sections. Flesh out your articles by adding more quotations (from your interview notes), additional references, and footnotes. Enhance each chapter by developing sidebars, charts, maps, graphs, quizzes, and/or summaries that can be placed strategically throughout the pages.

For my time management book's first chapter, "Understanding Time Management," I linked four features I had sold as part of my *Market Builder* series: "The Maxims of Time Management," "Understanding Life Phases," "The Management by Contract System," and "Self-generated Motivation." I added two sidebars, wrote a two-page commentary about how I, personally, became interested in time management, and then prepared seven transition paragraphs to aid the reader in getting from one subtopic to the next. In fewer than four hours I had organized, written, and typed an entire chapter. Two more weeks of working like that found me holding a completed book manuscript!

Step 6: Sell the Book Manuscript
Naturally, your next move is to sell your book. The process is simple. Study the markets until you come up with five book publishers who have a track record for publishing the kind of book you have written.

Send to one publisher at a time the following items: a cover letter, a typed table of contents, a detailed table of contents containing one paragraph of explanation about each chapter, two completed chapters, and a stamped, self-addressed envelope. (We discussed this in detail in the previous chapter's section "Writing Book Proposals.")

That cover letter at the top of the stack of materials will be your clincher. Explain in it that you have sold X number of articles on your book's topic; this proves not only that you are qualified to write on the subject but also that there is obvious reader interest in it. Enclose several published samples from your series and freelance sales.

In my own case, after having written twelve articles on time management and made seventeen reprint sales of those articles, I contacted Bobbs-Merrill Publishing Company with my book proposal for *Staying Ahead of Time.* I was offered a contract, and the book was released a year later.

Step 7: Sell Excerpts from the Book

Once your book appears in print, your next move is to sell excerpts from it. Excerpts put extra cash into your hands in addition to helping to promote your book.

There are several ways to sell excerpts. You or your publisher can send review copies to magazine editors and suggest certain chapters that might be appropriate for their readers. I did this with *Essence,* and the editor bought the excerpt rights to chapter two of my book ("The Days of Your Life," March 1982).

You also can write condensations of your chapters, hitting all the high points, and then submit these excerpts for sale to magazines. I did this with *Writer's Digest* ("The Time of Your Life," August 1982) and *Optical Management* ("Time Is on Your Side," March 1983) and *Young Ambassador* ("Time Warp," May 1984).

Sometimes you can even sell excerpts of your excerpts! After the excerpt from my book appeared in *Writer's Digest,* the editor of *Reader's Digest* paid me $50 to reprint one paragraph of my article in that magazine's "Points to Ponder" column (March 1983). Similarly, *Leader's Magazine* bought a 750-word excerpt from one of the 2,000-word articles in my series for *Market Builder.*

Step 8: Develop a Spin-Off Topic

Once your book is selling and is establishing you as an expert on that topic, begin working on a new series of articles on a closely related topic. This saves you research time, builds on your established reputation, and enables your publisher to promote your books in units or sets.

After publishing *Staying Ahead of Time,* a book on how to make the most of one's time, I wrote *Positive Workaholism,* a book on how to make one's work time more productive. It began as a double series of articles: one series in *Market Builder* and a different series in *Shop Talk.* That book later outsold my previous book four to one. Why? Because my name was already established in the field by the time the new book was released. Success compounds success.

When you look at a giant salami, you realize the only way to eat it all is to slice it and eat it one slice at a time. A book can be written the same way. Slice it into a lot of little articles, and you will be able to handle it like the salami. And that's no baloney.

EVALUATING ROYALTIES

I would like to conclude this section on marketing by assuming that since you will be getting into print, you will need some advice on how to assess a book publisher's royalty statement. There is nothing more frustrating and nerve-racking than waiting those long months between the time your book manuscript is accepted for publication and the day it is finally released. When the printed book finally arrives, you exist in a euphoric state for at least a month.

And then a new waiting period begins between the time your book is released and the day your first royalty check arrives (anywhere from 90 to 450 days later, depending on the terms of your contract).

Finally, the check arrives. With wide eyes you tear open the envelope. Your mind races. You have been on the road promoting the book at writers' conferences, autograph parties, bookstores, and libraries. The book has received favorable reviews, and you have written to all the relatives you have in six different states telling them to buy copies.

There is no way this royalty check can be less than $5,000, you tell yourself. Who knows? It may even be for $7,000 or $10,000.

With anticipation you draw the check close to your eyes. You stare.

Suddenly, your squinted eyes glare in horror.

You gasp and stammer, "Only $107? That's impossible."

Nevertheless, there it is in black and white.

What do you do now? Must you accept it as it is or are there ways to demand a recount? Experienced writers handle this situation in two ways:

1. Insist that an "examination of books of account" clause be inserted into each book contract before it is signed.

2. File a royalty assessment sheet each time a questionable royalty statement arrives.

In regard to the first step, it is wise to ask that a paragraph be added to each book contract that will give you access to the publisher's bookkeeping records detailing sales of your book or books. Here is an example of such a paragraph:

> The Author, upon written request, may examine the books of account of the Publisher insofar as they relate to the Literary Work. Such examination shall be at the Author's expense unless errors of accounting amounting to five percent (5%) or more of the total sums accrued to the Author shall be found to the Author's disadvantage, in which case the reasonable cost of the examination shall be borne by the Publisher and payment of the amount due shall be made within thirty (30) days thereafter.

In regard to the second step, it is a good idea to keep a supply of royalty assessment sheets (see section at the end of this chapter) on hand. These generic forms list all possible areas you might have questions about. Simply make a check mark by the area in question and then forward the sheet to the accounting department of your book's publishing company. If you do not receive a reply within two weeks, place a call to the editor you usually work with and make an oral request for a bookkeeping report to be sent to you.

Many times authors are shocked by their royalty checks because they have not carefully read their contracts before signing them. For example, if a publisher offers you a 10 percent royalty on book sales, does that mean 10 percent of the retail price or the wholesale price or the total amount of money earned by the book? As you can imagine, the range of earnings in these three instances can vary substantially. Likewise, sometimes new writers forget that the advance money they were paid has to be worked off before any new royalties will be paid. Also, many give-away books (for review purposes) or books sold at a steep discount to buying groups mean no royalty or a small percentage back to author (depending on the contract) on those books. So, read your contract carefully, insert an examination clause in it, and file assessment sheets when in doubt about royalties.

CONCLUSION

In closing, I would like to share this short note of encouragement. As the director of a university writing program, it is my joy to help beginning writers enhance their writing and marketing skills. Many, however, enter the program with dreams of becoming rich and famous writers in a very short time. Sorry, it just doesn't work that way—as with everything else in life.

Like all other professions, writing requires some sweat equity. Concert musicians have to practice daily for years before they are ready for professional recitals. Surgeons spend a dozen years in college and residency programs before they are ready to go into private practice. Athletes discipline their bodies for many years before they can compete in the Olympics.

As a writer, you, too, will have to discipline and train yourself. Reading and studying this book has been a giant step toward your goal of becoming a published author. Now, maintain that momentum. Read other books about writing; join a writers' club in your city; attend writers' conferences; take night-school journalism classes at your area college; subscribe to the leading periodicals for writers; keep a journal; write to magazines and ask for guidelines for writers; expand your vocabulary; join an on-line writers' chat room; develop and propose an idea for a column for your hometown newspaper. In short, let this book be the *beginning* of your writing career. Don't set it aside and say, "Well, that was fun, but now I have nowhere to go." Opportunities abound. Seek and you will find. If you are convinced that it is your life's goal to become a published writer, then do all you can to make that dream come true.

Along the way, however, do not forget how much *fun* it is to write. So, as the title of this book implies, you should also make the writing you love one of your priorities. Never lose the joy of writing. *That* is what keeps you returning to it. Write on!

Charlene B. Churchill
222 Second Avenue
Littleville, Ohio 46106
Phone/Fax:
E-mail:
December 16, 2004

Lois I. Davis, Managing Editor
Nazarene News
800 Trailblazer Road
Little Rock, Arkansas 60164

Dear Mrs. Davis:

I am interested in becoming a regional correspondent for the *Nazarene News.* I live in mid-Ohio and have both the time and accessibility to cover news throughout this area. I am a member of Main Street Nazarene Church, where I write the weekly church bulletin.

I am twenty-nine years old and am married and have one child, age ten. I am not employed out of my house and, thus, would have time to visit area churches throughout the week to gather news.

During high school I served two years as a reporter for the school newspaper. I graduated from Buckeye Community College with a two-year degree in English three years ago. I've written seven freelance articles this year that have been published in area newspapers and two religious magazines. Sample copies of three of my published articles are enclosed.

If I can be of service to you in the near future, I would enjoy hearing from you at your convenience. Thank you.

Respectfully yours,

(Mrs.) Charlene B. Churchill

CBC/cbc
Enclosure

ROYALTY ASSESSMENT SHEET

Dear Publisher,

I am in receipt of your recent royalty statement for my book *(book title here)* by *(author's name here).* Please supply me with the following information omitted in your statement and provide for it in future accountings:

_____ Title:

_____ Author:

_____ Edition: _____ Retail Price:

_____ Accounting Period Covered by the Statement:

_____ Initial Publication Date:

_____ Size of Printings: _____ First:

_____ Subsequent:

Sales This Period:

Royalty Rate %	Royalty Base %	Copies Sold	Copies Returned	Net Copies	Royalty Earned $

_____ Regular   _____ Mail Order

_____ Wholesale   _____ Special

Discount _____ %   _____ Canada

_____ %   Discount _____ %

_____ %   _____ %

                          _____ %

_____ Export

_____ Remaindered

Discount _____ %

_____ %

_____ %

Other Earnings (reprints, book clubs, serial, foreign, other):

Units	Rate %	Amount $	Author's Share

_____ (Source)

_____ Copy of Licensee's Statement:

_____ Total Copies Sold Last Period:

_____ Total Copies Sold This Period:

_____ Total Copies Sold to Date:

_____ Deductions Properly Itemized (advances, unearned balance, book purchases, etc.) with attached statement, where applicable:

_____ % Held as Reserve Against Returns:

DENNIS E. HENSLEY holds four university degrees in English, including a Ph.D. in linguistics and literature from Ball State University. He is the author of thirty-one books, including *Millennium Approaches* (Avon) and *Write on Target* (The Writer, Inc.). His more than 3,000 published freelance articles have appeared in more than 150 religious and secular magazines, including *Reader's Digest, Modern Bride, Essence, Writer's Journal, The Writer, ABA Journal, Lawyer's Magazine, Baptist Bulletin, Purpose Magazine, The War Cry, Evangel, The Christian Communicator, Fellowship Today, Live,* and *Success.*

Dr. Hensley also served for twenty-two years as a regional correspondent for *Writer's Digest,* writing more than 100 features for that magazine. He currently serves as a contributing editor for six national magazines.

Each year Dr. Hensley lectures at more than thirty writers' workshops and conferences. He has been a keynote speaker several times at the Midwest Writer's Workshop, American Christian Writers' Workshops, the Florida Suncoast Writers' Workshop, St. David's Christian Writers' Conference, the Mount Hermon Christian Writers' Conference, and the Sandy Cove Christian Writer's Conference, among many others. Dr. Hensley is a professor of English at Taylor University's Fort Wayne campus where he directs the Professional Writing program.

Dr. Hensley and his wife, Rose, have two children and reside in Fort Wayne, Indiana.